Life Lessons from
Esther

Life Lessons from
Esther

Penny Henderson

A Division of WINEPRESS PUBLISHING

Pleasant Word (a division of WinePress Publishing, PO Box 428, Enumclaw, WA 98022) functions only as book publisher. As such, the ultimate design, content, editorial accuracy, and views expressed or implied in this work are those of the author.

ISBN 1-4141-0409-X
Library of Congress Catalog Card Number: 2005901210

Dedication

This book is dedicated to
my dear husband, John,
from whom I have learned so much
and whose patience and generosity
have made it possible.

CONTENTS

Acknowledgements

Many thanks are due my friends Carol Anderson and Marilyn Anderes, who read and critiqued these lessons as I wrote them, saving me from many foolish errors and omissions. I am especially grateful to my "living concordance," Carol. If you find a chapter and verse citation that is wrong, you may be sure I didn't call her for that one.

I am also grateful to members of my small group who often helped me brainstorm: Dorothea Saavedra, Mary Jane Stauffer, Chris Santo, Diane Pell, Linda Gibson, Georgianna Hoover, Joanie Haydn, Jane Hurd, Laura Hayes, Stephanie Miles, Valerie Archer, Ann Macomber, and Cecelia Garcia. My friends Bonnie Upchurch and Melanie Saderholm reviewed much of the material and provided valuable suggestions.

FOREWORD

In 1999, my friend, Bev Gould, and I started a study to see how a number of biblical characters went about counseling the people for whom they were responsible before God. We did it because Bev was going back to school to be a counselor.

We started with Mordecai and how he counseled Esther, then moved on to Elijah's teaching of Elisha, Moses' training up of Joshua, and Jesus with the disciples. But my heart kept going back to Esther. We had expected to find little beyond the famous "perhaps you were put here for such a time as this" and found instead a book rich in wisdom, once you get under and beyond the surface story.

I first put these lessons together as a series of talks, and at the very first one a listener challenged me about not addressing a whole area of concern. Some liberal Christian and secular critics say the Book of Esther is mistakenly included in the canon, because the name of God is never mentioned. Their second point is that the Jewish people who are the characters in the story were not practicing Jews or they would have gone back to Israel by the time the events of Esther took place. Finally, they say that Esther, if properly raised in a traditional Jewish home, would never have found herself in the king's harem in the first place.

I don't think any of that holds water. It betrays a basic misunderstanding of the human condition. We are a fallen people. Even Paul said that whatever he should do, he somehow left undone, and the very thing he shouldn't do was often what he found himself doing. I would hesitate to assume that on that basis Paul was not a committed Christian. I would also not assume that Rabbi Daniel Lapin is not a practicing Jew because he has not returned to Israel in the years since 1948, so I don't think we can assume that about Mordecai.

I'm quite sure we cannot conclude that all the Jewish girls swept into Hitler's brothels were from secular families and had not been raised in the fear and admonition of the Lord, so that is not a safe assumption about Esther, either.

As far as Esther's inclusion in the Bible being a mistake, I don't think God makes mistakes. Our Bible, our love letter from God, is so multi-layered and multi-dimensional that many things can be learned from just one passage. What I have searched for in writing these lessons is not the big sweeping theme of the Book of Esther (which is God's providence for His people) but the more everyday "how-to-live" sidelights.

In each lesson, I have started with an insight gleaned from the story of Esther and then ranged to and fro through the Bible, the works of great Christian men and women, and my own experience to put flesh on that skeletal central thought.

My prayer is that it speaks to each reader at the point of some need and that God will use it to help meet that need. By using the leader's guide (available by email at sweetbriar@aol.com; put "leader's guide" on the subject line) and the study questions for each chapter at the end of the book, it can become an effective group study.

Chapter 1

FAITHFULNESS

The first lesson we see Esther's cousin, Mordecai, teaching is faithfulness. The second, explored in the next chapter, is loyalty. They seem close in meaning. As I thought about the difference, it seemed to me that faithfulness was to a task and loyalty was to a person. Webster's Dictionary[1] defines *loyal* two ways: 1) faithful in allegiance to ones lawful government, or 2) faithful to a private person to whom fidelity is held to be due.

It defines *faithful* three ways: 1) full of faith (duh!); 2) the second definition refers to the marital type of faithfulness, which is really embodied in number three; 3) firm adherence to promises or duty.

[handwritten margin notes: Loyal Person / Faithful Task]

The difference here isn't huge but seems important. It is interesting that while loyalty is shown *to* a government or person, it is shown *by* being faithful in one's duty.

Here are a few statements that may clarify what I mean.

- You are faithful to keep your marriage vows because you are loyal to your husband.
- Because you are loyal to our government and to God whose Word gives the government legitimacy, you faithfully pay your income tax.
- Because you are loyal to your friend, you are faithful to keep her confidences.

How Was Mordecai Faithful?

We see Mordecai demonstrating faithfulness in several ways. The first is in Esther 2:11 when Esther has been swept into the king's harem and Mordecai has cautioned her not to tell anyone who her people are. Then verse eleven tells us that "every day Mordecai walked in front of the court of the harem, to learn how Esther was and how she fared."

That was faithfulness, not a sporadic, occasional letter but going daily to where she was, keeping track of her progress. He didn't just give the good advice and walk away, hoping it would all turn out for the best. He stayed on top of it in case she should have further need of him.

This is how God treats *us*. He didn't just give us His Word in the Bible and walk away hoping we'd read it. He first sent His Son, the Living Word, to make sure we had the means to reach Him and then the Holy Spirit to chase us down the days and down the nights, thereby motivating us to reach Him. And He is always there as a refuge if we will turn to Him.

In Psalm 37:40, David says:

The Lord helps them and delivers them; He delivers them from the wicked, and saves them, because they take refuge in him.

Psalm 46:1-3 reads:

God is our refuge and strength, a very present help in trouble. Therefore we will not fear though the earth should change, though the mountains shake in the heart of the sea; though its waters roar and foam, though the mountains tremble with its tumult.

This kind of faithfulness is what we are meant to be growing toward as we become more Christlike. The whole process is about drawing close to God. That process isn't easy. C. S. Lewis talked about the word "Christian" meaning "little Christ." He assured us that becoming "little Christs" was not a necessarily a pleasant process when he gave us this analogy: "It may be hard for an egg to turn into a bird; it would be a jolly sight harder for it to learn to fly while remaining an egg. We are like eggs at present. You cannot go on being just an ordinary decent egg. You must be hatched or go bad"[2].

What Does Faithfulness Look Like?

Mordecai's lesson is that faithfulness is not easy. It's a daily thing. It's not just giving wise counsel but dutifully doing the followup.

This faithful followup is one of the most demanding and frustrating aspects of parenting. My mother had a very effective followup system. It involved a stern look and a raised eyebrow. She could modify my behavior across any crowded room with that eyebrow. Its message was often, "Remember what I said."

We see Jesus using this technique on Peter. Earlier, Jesus had told Peter, to Peter's aghast disbelief, that before the cock crowed, Peter would deny Him three times. The story is in Luke 22:56–61a.

> Then a maid, seeing him as he sat in the light and gazing at him, said, "This man also was with him." But he denied it, saying, "Woman, I do not

know him." And a little later someone else saw him and said, "You also are one of them." But Peter said, "Man, I am not." And after an interval of about an hour still another insisted, saying, "Certainly this man also was with him; for he is a Gallilean." But Peter said, "Man, I do not know what you are saying." And immediately, while he was still speaking, the cock crowed. And the Lord turned and looked at Peter.

Across that crowded, emotionally-charged courtyard, it only took "the look" to bring Peter to the realization of what he was doing.

As a parent, "the look" is an invaluable tool, but I know from experience that it eventually loses its impact, about the time your child develops "a look" of his or her own to use on your grandchildren. The faithful verbal followup is a more permanent fixture. It changes, but it never ends. The progression might sound something like this.

"I'm so sorry your tummy hurts. Let's rock a while. Mommy will pray for you. I love you. You're my precious child."

"What did you think of the way Susie talked to her brother? Do you think that's the way God wants brothers and sisters to act? What do you think would be the right way to act if your brother did what her's did?"

"Don't forget to brush your teeth."

"Let's pray for Daddy, he's going to have a hard day."

"I'm sorry you disagree, but there absolutely *must* be a shower after football practice and before dinner."

"You seem to be having a lot of trouble with physics. Do you think a tutor would help?"

"Honey, don't be tempted in all the rush to skip the pre-marital counseling."

"I know it's hard with three toddlers, but I think you'll find it's easier to connect with them if you make time to keep yourself connected to God."

"I'm so weak now, I can't help you the way I used to, but even now, I pray for you. I love you. You are my precious child."

Praying Faithfully

Praying is the most important part. Being faithful to pray for your children is the best gift you can give them. In his book on Esther, Chuck Swindoll challenges us about praying for our children when he writes: "Do you stand beside the bedside of your little girl and boy, praying: 'Lord raise her up to be courageous, like Esther; cultivate in him the heart of Mordecai. Speak your message theough their lips. Carry out your great plan through the life of this precious child of mine'?"[3]

My friend Carol Anderson advised in a long-ago Bible study that we should pray for our children's future spouses. Obviously, we didn't know then who they would be. It has been a blessing to me to know now that I was praying for my dear daughter-in-law, Kelly, all those years before I even knew her. But it isn't about getting a blessing for yourself. It's about being faithful to do what God says He wants us to do pray at all times.

One of my advisors on these lessons pointed out that one of the hardest, yet most important, tasks of faithfulness that a parent has is to a grown but wayward child. The faithfulness consists of continuing to love them, to pray for them, to speak the truth in love, and to give them to God.

We are shown Mordecai being faithful to pray. He didn't just *tell* Esther he would fast, he organized the community, they fasted, and, we can safely assume, prayed. It does not say they prayed, but the only logical reason to fast in that situation was to facilitate prayer. Here we see one of the subtle ways God enters a book where His name is not mentioned. One only fasted in order to pray, and why pray if no one is listening?

Being Faithful to Parents

Proverbs 15:22 tells us that "without counsel plans go wrong, but with many advisors they succeed." So as I prepared these studies, I gave my rough drafts to several people for comment.

My friend, Stephanie, pointed out that I had missed the faithfulness that is due our parents. I suppose I missed it because there is no actual parent/child ralationship portrayed in Esther, but at Steph's pointer, I quickly spotted the fact that Esther showed that kind of respect to Mordecai, who was her surrogate father. She was obediant. He said, "Don't mention your heritage," so she didn't. It says in 2:20b: "for Esther obeyed Mordecai just as when she was brought up by him."

Her obediance was nothing new. Because she had trained herself in obediance and respect in the small things of everyday life, she was accustomed to saying, "Yes, Cousin." We are given no glimpse into Mordecai's old age, but I think Esther was probably there taking care of him.

As adults, the responsibility of our obedience shifts. Our major duty lies first in obedience to God, then to those in positions of authority over us: husband, government, employer, etc. So, while *obedience* to our parents isn't the focal point it once was, respect and faithfulness still are. The commandment says, "Honor your father and mother…. that your days may be prolonged, and that it might go well with you….."

As adults, we do that by keeping in touch, by teaching our children to love and repect them, and by filling their legitimate needs to the best of our ability. I'm not talking about their unreasonable desires. The mother who is hurt if you don't call *every* day or spend *every* Sunday afternoon with her needs to do a little growing up herself, but her need to maintain a relationship with you and your family is real. Not all of us are blessed with parents as wise and faithful as Mordecai, but you can break the cycle by being faithful to them anyway and by modeling that before your children. Sometimes it is hard, but you can figure out a way to be faithful to your parents if you pray and try. I have seen a number of people with very difficult parents figure out ways to be faithful to them.

The Faithful Role Model

It's a little easier to be faithful to pray and to follow up in the area of friendship, but I know that even there I have failed many times. I'm talking about this sort of thing: Your friend calls and asks you to pray about a difficult time she is having. Do you then faithfully include her in your daily talk with God? Do you remember to call and ask her how it's going, assure her you are praying, and ask if there is anything else you can do to help? Honest answers to that probably range from "sometimes" to "usually." My honest answer is, "More often than I used to, but not as much as I should."

Another example of faithfulness brought to my attention is the faithfulness of a dog. That's the kind of faithfulness we owe our friends. The "old faithful," always there; call, and he comes kind.

Being faithful to pray and to follow up is also important in a mentoring relationship, and do remember that it doesn't have to be *labeled* mentoring for you to have a responsibility before God. The child next door whose parents are inattentive and who loves to hang out at your house has been given to you. Be faithful.

The difficult employee has been given to you. Be faithful.

The younger or older woman helping you in a ministry has been given to you. Be faithful.

The soccer team you coach has been given to you. Be faithful.

My friend Mary Jane Stauffer gives a lot of credit for the fact that she grew up to walk with God to some faithful Sunday school teachers who brought her little encouraging gifts and would even pick her up to make sure she didn't miss out on anything.

A story I heard from Carol Anderson typifies this. When she was in high school, there was a woman who took her under her wing and discipled her. As she left to go into ministry as a pastor's wife, this woman told her, "I will be praying for you." They kept in touch but not close touch—a couple of letters or cards a year. Forty-six years later, the woman's daughter wrote Carol and said that as she was in her final illness her mother worried because she didn't have her prayer list with her in the hospital, so the daughter brought it to her and the mother asked her to read it aloud so she could pray. Carol was still on it. What a saint! What a faithful mentor!

Faithfulness In Marriage

Finally, we come to faithfulness in marriage. This is so much more than lack of physical infidelity. There is also a little-considered betrayal that might be called emotional infidelity. It could be that you form such a strong link with a friend—man or woman that you are sharing your intimate emotions of fear, joy, spiritual growth, anxiety, etc. with them *instead* of with your mate.

I'm not implying there is anything wrong with having a close friend. There are some things that only another woman can really understand and relate to, but you do need to guard against letting that close friendship *replace* what you should be sharing with your husband. I cannot think of an instance where having that level of emotional intimacy with another man would be wise.

Faithfulness in marriage also involves controlling your tongue in public. This principle aplies everywhere—in every relationship—not just marriage. While it's fine to laugh with your friend over the fact that your husband will walk all the way across the room only to drop his clothes on the floor at the foot of the hamper, it's not being faithful to discuss the details of your sex life, or his spiritual struggles, or anything else he might rightly consider would remain between the two of you. It involves controlling your tongue in private, not criticizing him to or in front of the children, not making him feel stupid or inadequate.

The sin of gossip fits in here. We are to love and pray for our enemies, not gossip and seek revenge. How much more then should we not be telling negative stories about our spouse or our friends?

Once you've started being able *not* to say certain kinds of things, you can start working on what you *should* say. Give him credit in public for the things he does right. Do it especially if he's there to hear it.

At home, thank him for what he does to help, even when it doesn't seem like much. We all need to feel appreciated, and the helpful action seemingly unnoticed is not apt to be repeated. All this advice applies to roommates, fellow workers, etc.

Keeping Promises

Faithfulnes also involves doing what you say you'll do. Mordecai didn't just tell Esther that the community would fast, he went out, organized the people, and got them to fast. Make lists, put post-it notes on the steering wheel, do whatever it takes to remember to do those things you have told your husband, or anyone else, that you would accomplish.

This was one of my major downfalls as a young wife. I am very forgetful, and on top of that, I have a tendency to procrastinate. If I *did* remember the task, I would think that I would do it when I finished "this," but when I was finished, I would have forgotten it again. This explains but doesn't excuse my faithlessness. If I had been able to see where it would lead, I would surely have tried a lot harder to find ways to defeat my natural tendencies.

My husband forgets almost as many things as I do now, but back then, he had a mind like a steel trap and always assumed, since forgetting was not something he had any experience with, that if I didn't make the phone call or run the errand he had asked me to that I had purposely not done it just to make his life harder.

That situation led me further into sin, because rather than have him think I wanted him to be aggravated and frustrated, I would make up all sorts of wild stories about why I hadn't gotten things done.

Well—that's pretty euphemistic—, what I did was I lied.

In James we are taught that "desire when it has concieved gives birth to sin; and sin when it is full grown brings forth death". As with so much in Scripture, this truth applies on many levels

My desire to have Johny think well of me led me to the sin of telling lies, and that sin brought about the numbing, and finally the death, of my conscience, until at last it didn't even seem wrong, just expedient. It has taken a lot of work by the Holy Spirit—none of which was pleasurable for me to resurrect me from that death and turn me back into an honest person.

It is so much easier to be faithful in the first place than to have to go back and fix it. Often, you can't. What a joy it would be if you could learn from Mordecai's example and from my mistakes. The first step is to pray. Ask God to *show* you where you are being unfaithful and ask Him to help you change in areas you already know about.

The next lesson will explore loyalty. There will be a lot of times when the examples I use from Mordecai's story to demonstrate loyalty will also show faithfulness, because, as we have discussed, loyalty is demonstrated by being faithful.

To say it another way, we reach the high goal of becoming a loyal person by walking up the steps of being faithful. The faithful daily action of showing up outside the palace shows us that Mordecai was loyal to Esther.

DISCUSSION QUESTIONS

1. Does it bother you that God's name is never mentioned in the Book of Esther? Why, or why not?

_____

_____

_____

_____

2. Who has modeled faithfulness for you?

_____

_____

_____

_____

3. Who might be looking to you as a model?

_____

_____

_____

_____

4. Where have you succeeded at being faithful?

_____

_____

_____

_____

5. Write down some practical ways to start chang-
    ing in the areas where you have not succeeded.
    Share, if you are studying in a group.

    _____

    _____

    _____

    _____

6. What does the author say is even more important
    than learning to live the details of your life in a
    way pleasing to God?

    _____

    _____

    _____

    _____

7. Talk about how you can keep this balance clear
    in your mind.

    _____

    _____

    _____

    _____

- Significance of seven
- Castration / eunich

CHAPTER 2

LOYALTY

We saw in the last lesson that while faithfulness and loyalty are similar, they are not twins. Being faithful is a way to express loyalty, which is defined as allegiance to a person or government.

In this chapter, we will look at three kinds of loyalty to family, to country, and to God, because those are the ones I saw embodied in the Book of Esther. We will also give a passing nod to loyalty to truth, employers, and friends.

We will discuss conscience, because it's your well-developed conscience that helps you discern to where, to what, and to whom you should be loyal.

Family Loyalty

The first glimpse we get of the quality of Mordecai's character is when we are told in Esther 2:7 that he raised his orphaned cousin as his own child. In my mind, maybe as a result of long-ago Sunday school lessons, Mordecai was always an old man. Perhaps he really was, but the fact that he was Esther's cousin, not her uncle or her grandfather, leaves open the very real possibility that he was only a few years older than she was. If that was the case, no earthly rebuke would have followed if he had shirked this responsibility, but he didn't. That is an example of family loyalty.

First Timothy 5:3–8 cautions us that there is a religious duty that we owe our family. The family is God's first line of defense against poverty; then, lacking family, the Church. Here's how the first part of it reads in The Message: "Take care of widows who are destitute. If a widow has family members to take care of her, let them learn that religion begins at their own doorstep, and that they should pay back with gratitude some of what they have received. This pleases God immensely." It goes on a few verses later: "Anyone who neglects to care for family members in need repudiates the faith. That's worse than refusing to believe in the first place."[1]

This caution to take care of family is repeated throughout the Bible. All the Jewish rules about brothers marrying their brothers' widows were set up to give structure to the idea that members of families were to take care of each other and that nobody was to be cheated out of their inheritance. We see this demonstrated clearly in the Book of Ruth. Boaz had to clear his marriage to Ruth through the closer relative who bore the responsibility of taking care of her. And Ruth, a Moabite, who didn't even have the law as a guide, nevertheless listened to her conscience and stuck by her mother-in-law, Naomi, not allowing her to make the difficult journey back to her home all alone. This loyalty was later rewarded when Boaz married her and she became the great-grandmother of King David. The Bible makes it clear that the strength of a nation is in its families.

The Importance of Conscience

Even people who did not know the God of Abraham, Isaac, and Jacob used to be able to consult their conscience, or "natural law," to guide their conduct as Ruth did. Chuck Colson, in a speech to the graduating class of 2000 at Wheaton College,[2] talked about the modern-day break down of conscience.

Mr. Colson quotes many sources and makes his argument convincingly. I will quote only his wrap up.

Thus it is that we no longer think of conscience as an inner moral compass, calibrated to true north; it is rather like a Ouija board that points in the direction we choose. In which event the familiar expression, "let your conscience be your guide," which might in an earlier time have been a reasonable adage, is now the most dangerous thing we can say to someone. It is an invitation to do wrong and feel good about it.

This is a major reason why it is incumbent upon us as Christians to study the Bible. Our teachers, leaders, the popular press, some churches, and maybe even our parents have not only failed to lay a proper groundwork for conscience but have meticulously laid the false one that "if it feels right, how can it be wrong?" A thorough knowledge of God's Word is the only stone we have with which to re-sharpen our consciences and reclaim them as useful tools.

Proverbs 14:12 says it all: "There is a way which seems right to man, but its end is the way to death." To find God's way, which leads to life, we need to know His Word. Since Mordecai knew not to bow down to anyone but God, I think we can safely assume he knew the rest of the Law of Moses and that that is what kept his conscience well-tuned. It was certainly sharp when it came to loyalty.

My friend Carol Anderson says that Proverbs 17:17 has always been a watchword in their home. It says, "A brother was born for adversity." They taught their children that you should always be loyal to family and friends, helping in times of trouble, which isn't the same as saying you must always approve of their behavior.

When I tell my grandchildren that wonderful biblical story, "The Three little Pigs," I always end up with "and the moral of the story is twofold." (Yes, I really talk to them that way—they are, of course, exceptional children.) "The first part of the moral is it's usually worth it to work a little harder and a little longer and do the job right. The second part of the moral is be nice to your brother—you may need him later." This is not at all the right reason for being loyal to your brother, but it does seem to stick in their heads.

So What If I Don't?

When this principle of taking family obligations seriously is ignored, the consequences can be disastrous. We see this acted out all around us today. There are also some excellent biblical examples. The first one to pop into my mind is the way David failed to teach his sons as a father should. It says in 1 Kings 1:6, the story of David's rebellious son, Adonijah, that "His father had never at any time displeased

him by asking, 'why have you done thus and so?'"
Of all David's sons, David seems to have taught and
admonished only Solomon. The latter part of David's
reign was troubled and unstable for two reasons: 1)
the sin he committed in taking Bathsheba and killing Uriah; and 2) because he had not taken a hand
in disciplining his sons.

Another terrible story that was the result of a
breakdown of family loyalty is the history of Joseph
whose brothers first threw him down a well and then
sold him into slavery. Of course, what the brothers meant for evil God used for good. And Joseph,
seeing the hand of God in the whole thing, did not
abandon his own family loyalty, even in the face of
extreme provocation. It wound up being the story of
the foundation of the twelve tribes of Israel. Holding
on to God's principles for right living even when
others are throwing them out the window may well
set you up to be mightily used by God.

Loyalty To Country

Mordecai's smoothly functioning conscience
also led him to be loyal to his king. We are not told
exactly what post he held, but the fact that he was
"sitting in the gate" is a clue that he was a servant
of the king. In the course of his duties he learned of
a plot to harm the king.

"Lay hands on," in chapter two, verse twenty-one, probably means "kill." It could mean, "drop a piano on," as in the "Veggie Tales" (a children's cartoon) version, but my money is on "kill." Mordecai passed this information on to Esther, who told the king, and the plotters were arrested. Part of the aftermath of this was the promotion of Haman to a position of authority, second only to the king.

This brings us to a hard lesson: the immediate results of being loyal and doing what is right are not always to our advantage. Haman being put into a position of more power was a very bad thing for Mordecai and potentially for Esther if Haman had found out she was a Jew. It is important to be loyal just because it's right and not because of the expected results.

In the preface to her book, *More Precious Than Silver*,[3] Joni Erickson Tada talks from Psalm 12:6 about God's Word being like silver: "The words of the Lord are promises that are pure, silver refined in a furnace on the ground, purified seven times." She says that unlike gold, silver needs no impurities in it to bond, and it has the unique capacity to kill bacteria. Man looks upon the outward appearance (gold), but God judges the heart. We need to be checking our hearts, keeping the "clean silver" of God's Word there, discerning whether we are choosing to do things based on results or based on what's right.

I'm not sure Mordecai had any idea what trouble would ensue as a result of his action, but many times we *can* see the difficulties that lay ahead if we follow our conscience and do what is right. These potential difficulties must not be the deciding factor.

A few examples: One, if, in a moment of weakness, you have told a lie about something and everybody bought it, it will cause a lot more trouble for you to go back and set the record straight than to just keep going. Even though you may have repented and resolved never to do it again, the right thing is to confess the lie and set the record straight. Be loyal to the truth.

A second example: If you acquire evidence that a coworker is embezzling funds, the right thing to do is to report it. This may cause you all kinds of trouble. Now, here, a little balance is needed. In The Message, Proverbs 30:10 reads, "Don't blow the whistle on your fellow workers behind their backs. They'll accuse you of being underhanded and you'll be the guilty one." Think back to your childhood. Do you remember the difference between being a tattletale—"Mommy, he took my ball" and telling what needed to be told: "Mommy, my brother is eating dog poo"?

It's a fine line, but one reliable rule is that if it is *your* rights or *your* pride that are being stepped on, pray and let it go. If, on the other hand, there is the potential for some one else to be hurt, including your employer, you need to tell.

That still leaves a seemingly "gray area" where discernment is needed. James says that if you lack wisdom you should ask God for it in faith and He will give it to you (James 1:5). So pray at all times but most especially when you are operating in the gray area. It's not really gray. You just don't currently have on the right glasses. You need to gain God's perspective. That comes with prayer.

A third example is that the family loyalty you display when you discipline your children—teaching them the difference between right and wrong and the truth that actions have consequences is a lot of trouble. It requires not only quality time but *quantity* time. And this is one area where you really can't go back and put it right later, as David found out to his sorrow. If you don't teach these things early and in an evenhanded and consistent manner, there is no way to jump in at age fifteen and set it right. At that point, they will have to learn the hard way. As my friend Carol has said many times, "If you don't discipline your children, someone else will (their peers, the school system, the police), and *they* won't do it in love."

The Big Picture

The short term consequences of doing what is right—following a conscience that has been sharpened by immersing it in God's Word—can range from moderate discomfort to full-fledged disaster, but the long term results are always amazing.

In Mordecai's case, it was the record of what he had done about the assassination plot that later became the hinge to swing open the door revealing Haman's true nature to the king. It all worked out really well. In human, not eternal, terms, that isn't always the case.

Detrich Bonhoeffer, a patriotic German who loved his country, decided he loved God more. He stood against Hitler and for the gospel, and it cost him his life. From the point of view of those who loved him and were left behind, that was disaster. Looking from an eternal perspective, Detrich is with Jesus. As Paul said, "to live is Christ, and to die is gain" (Philippians 1:21). And, Bonhoeffer's life and writings have been an inspiration to many Christians in the half-century since then, and, should the Lord tarry, will continue to be for many more centuries.

If he had knuckled under to Hitler and towed the party line, all the truth and inspiration God had enabled him to write would have been smirched and viewed as the questionable ravings of a hypocrite.

Clearly, being loyal, doing what is right, and honing your conscience so you will know what that is does not always appear to turn out well. The eternal perspective is different, and the internal perspective is also. Exercising our loyalty to God, truth, country, employer, family, and friends is one of the ways we allow God to refine the silver of our hearts. Purification doesn't happen while we're sitting in a lawn chair drinking iced tea. It happens in the furnace.

Another biblical example of loyalty can be seen in a more positive story from the life of King David. Even when Saul was trying to kill him, David remained loyal. He had two chances to kill Saul but used each of them to demonstrate to his loyalty to the king. David's famous lament, "Thy glory, O Israel, is slain upon they high places! How are the mighty fallen!" (II Samuel 1:19), was not just for his friend, Jonathan, fallen in battle, but for his dead king—the very one who had hunted him and tried to kill him.

What Does That Look Like Now?

We have no king, but we have a country, so what are some of the ways we can show loyalty to our country today? I think the foremost way is to never waste our right to vote. Even in heated presidential elections, only a small percentage of Americans vote. And we really fall down on the job in the off years and in special local elections. I read somewhere that democracy will only work where there is a moral and educated citizenry. As Christians, we should be the citizens with the best grip on the meaning of "moral," that which conforms to what God says is right. In order to be loyal to our country we need to do the harder duty of staying informed, so we can make sound judgments. Then we need to actually go and vote. Never think again that your vote doesn't count—remember Florida.

And remember these amazing statistics from Chuck Swindoll:[4]

In 1645, one vote gave Oliver Cromwell control of England.

In 1776, one vote gave America the English language instead of German.

In 1845, one vote brought Texas into the union.

In 1941, one vote saved the selective service system just twelve weeks before Pearl Harbor.

Don't fall into a trap of inaction because of the fuzzy thinking that says "there is no good choice." For each office, one of the people on the ballot is going to be elected, and the way they do their job will probably impact your life. It's important who's on the school board. It matters who serves us in the state legislature. It is our job as loyal citizens to help make that decision. Sometimes it's easy and sometimes it seems to be choosing the lesser of two evils. Well, wouldn't you rather have the lesser one? It's our duty to help make the choice.

We also show loyalty to our country when we support causes we have judged to be righteous. We can do this financially by contributing to groups that are effectively lobbying the cause or by contributing to the campaign fund of a candidate who has his or her feet firmly on the right side of the issue.

Just as effective is calling or writing your own state or federal representatives and senators during the weeks leading up to an important vote. The most effective action is to pray. If all the Christians in this country were faithfully on their knees before God, interceding on behalf of our government, I believe the results would be astounding.

Second Chronicles 7:14 says, "if my people who are called by my name humble themselves, and pray and seek my face, and turn from their wicked ways, then I will hear from heaven, and will forgive their sin and heal their land."

A Loyal Spouse

We covered a lot in the last chapter about showing loyalty to your spouse by being faithful. I'll just add one story to that to reinforce the concept that both loyalty and faithfulness are due your spouse.

My daughter once said, "I don't understand people who are always complaining about their parents. You guys may not be perfect, but you're *mine*! I want my friends to think you're great." I think this is the essence of a loyal attitude, especially toward your husband: protective, working problems out other than in the public forum. I'm not saying some wise counsel isn't sometimes helpful, but seeking wise counsel is totally different from complaining endlessly to whoever will listen. That is the opposite of loyalty.

Loyalty to God

The last form of loyalty we see portrayed in Esther is loyalty to God. This is a huge subject. I am going to stick to only the aspects of it we see displayed in Esther. Don't be fooled and think I have covered the whole subject. I won't even manage to cover the three points I *am* going to address in anything like a complete way. Before starting this study I chose my theme verse from The Message version of Ephesians 3: "Here I am preaching and writing about things that are way over my head". With that in mind, the three aspects of loyalty to God I have gleaned from studying Esther are

1. Learning His ways,
2. Following His ways,

3. Remembering always to pray for strength and guidance.

Learning

We know from a couple of little things that Mordecai had learned God's ways. There is the fact that he knew not to bow down to anyone but God, and there is the fact that he knew he had a responsibility, according Mosaic Law, to take care of his family. We can, I think, safely assume he knew a lot more that just wasn't pertinent to the story.

How does that apply to our lives today? I think it is an area where a large majority of Christians fall short. I know I do. There was a story told in a study my small group did about how the FBI teaches people to recognize counterfeit money. They never have them look at the fake stuff. They study the real thing. That is the way the Lord intends to safeguard us from being ripped off by false prophets. He told us to write His Word on our hearts, and He says that all scripture is profitable for teaching and reproof. We are to be so familiar with what is from God that we instantly have our discernment hackles raised when we see something that isn't.

When my children were in grade school, I felt God was telling me to study the word "turn," which I found had a lot to do with balance. I used my concordance, I consulted friends, I read little study books that had the words "turn" or "balance" in the title. I found a lot of seemingly contradictory verses and tried to figure out through study of the context and comparing them to the rest of Scripture how it was that they represented balance. I'll share one set of them.

The first is the verse in Matthew from the Sermon on the Mount where Jesus says, "therefore do not be anxious, saying, 'What shall we eat', or 'What shall we drink?' or 'What shall we wear?' For the Gentiles seek all these things, and your heavenly Father knows that you need them all. But seek first his kingdom and his righteousness, and all these will be yours as well. Therefore, do not be anxious about tomorrow, for tomorrow will be anxious for itself" (Mathew 6:31-34). Compare that with the verse in Proverbs that says, "A little sleep, a little slumber, a little folding of the hands to rest and poverty will come upon you like a robber" (Proverbs 24: 33-34). Or in Second Thessalonians where it says that he who will not work shall not eat (II Thessalonians 3:10).

At first blush, these seem contradictory, but on closer inspection you find that they are teachings about different things. The verse in Matthew applies to the condition of our hearts, to where our attention is. It is a teaching about not fussing or worrying.

The other two are teachings about how to conduct ourselves. Our outward actions are addressed, not our inward attitudes. The balance here is to work hard with your body but keep your mind on God.

What if you only knew the verse from Proverbs about "a little sleep a little slumber"? How would that skew your walk? You would be very unbalanced. There's a good chance you would become bitter.

What if you only knew the verse from Matthew about letting tomorrow worry about itself? You would likely become an encumbrance to your family and to society. Balance is essential, and to achieve that balance, it is necessary to know what the Bible says.

The Word of God is so complex and so deep in layers of new learning to be gotten from it that we must never fool ourselves that we "know it now." A number of years ago, my pastor, Tim Webster, handed out a single sheet of paper listing the daily readings for going through the whole Bible in year. I decided to take up the challenge. I got terribly behind, but I kept sloshing away at it. When I got to Psalms, I made a running leap at trying to catch up, but I bogged down again in the Minor Prophets.

As Christmas approached, it seemed I would never make it, but I was determined to keep the promise I had made to God, and I did. I doubled up every day of December. On New Year's Eve, I had to read through 2 Peter; 1, 2, and 3 John; Jude; and the entire Book of Revelation, but I made it.

Before I started, I was sure that I had read all of the Bible at one time or another, just not in order, but I found out differently. There were things in there I had never seen. There was stuff in *Psalms* I had never seen. What a shock! Equally unexpected was the realization that reading it in order gave a new perspective and a new appreciation of the importance of context. And then, early New Year's day, feeling very smug and righteous, I went to the place where I have my quiet times and started praying and thanking the Lord for enabling me to finish what I had started, and I found that the Holy Spirit wasn't done with me. His still small voice was nudging, "Do you really think you got it all?" Well, of course not!

Reluctantly, I pulled out the now marked-up paper I had taken from Tim the year before and started again. I did better that time, never getting more than two or three days behind. And I was amazed to find that there were still things I'd never seen. By the third year, I was looking forward to seeing what God would show me this time. I'm still doing it. I think I will do this the rest of my life. That's how much of a blessing it has been.

Everyone is different (praise God), and I'm not trying to tell you that you should read through the

Bible every year for the rest of your life. I don't know how God wants you to study His Word, but I know that He wants you to. And I know that if you want to draw close to God, and if you want the gift of discernment, and if you want to be wise, you *need* to study it.

C. S. Lewis said, "If Christianity is not true then it is of no importance at all. If it is true, it is of ultimate importance. The only thing it can never be is of moderate importance"[5]. Knowing God's Word is not of moderate importance, either.

Following

James says, "but be doers of the word, and not hearers only, deceiving yourselves" (James 1:22). Mordecai was certainly a doer. He knew from the Word that he was supposed to take care of his cousin, so he did it. He knew he should be loyal to his king, so when he overheard the assassination plot, he acted.

One of the hardest lessons I've had to learn is that God is not apt to show me a second or a third illuminating truth until I've acted on the one He's already shown me. If He has held up before me— spot-lighted it in my mind and spirit Philippians 4:8, which says, "Finally brethren, whatever is true, whatever is honorable, whatever is just, whatever is pure, whatever is lovely, whatever is gracious, if there is <u>any excellence</u>, if <u>there is anything</u> worthy of praise, think about <u>these things</u>," and yet I have not quit reading the kind of fiction that is none of those things, what is that? Disobedience!

God doesn't honor disobedience. My friend Marilyn Anderes has a retreat ministry, and one of her talks centers around the time God descended to the top of the mountain and Moses went up to meet Him. The talk is titled, "Come Higher, There's More."

Well, you can't come higher by skipping over whole sections of the mountain or the staircase. Scotty can't beam you up. You have to climb one step at a time. God is watching, and His Word is the lamp unto our feet. Feet firmly on step six? OK, He will illuminate step seven. You have to act on what you've been taught.

I have a few different ways to occupy my mind while I'm driving. Sometimes I pray. More often I go over Scripture passages that I've memorized. I've been known to slip Elvis or the Beach Boys into the tape deck (especially, for some reason, in the spring, when driving with the windows down).

Once in a while I turn on our local all-news station to catch the weather and the latest headlines. More often than any of the others, I turn on the local Christian station, WAVA. One day I was in the car at an unusual time of day for me and I heard a preacher I'd never heard before, and he was *preaching*!

After listening a few minutes, I thought he was preaching works as more important than faith, which would have been way off, but he was so good I just kept listening, and soon found that he was right on. It was Tony Evans[6]. In his wrap up, he said something that really stuck with me. He said if all you want is heaven, then all you need is faith. But if you want any of the rewards of faith on this earth, you'd better put some legs under it—you'd better start acting on that faith. His example was great: David, he said, had plenty of faith that God could bring him victory over Goliath, but God didn't act to give that victory until David picked up the stones and threw them.

Calling Home

The third form of loyalty to God is keeping in touch. You need to call home and ask for guidance before you act. In the story of Esther, we are told that Esther asked Mordecai to get the entire Jewish population of Susa to fast before she took the irrevocable step of going in to see the king without having been called. She also fasted. The only reason for Jews to fast was to pray, so she under-girded her effort with three days of prayer and fasting.

How many times do we even forget to offer up a little ten-second "balloon" prayer before starting a new endeavor? Have we prayed mightily for our children, even perhaps through the night before their first day in school each year? I didn't. I think I said something like, "Please guard her through the day, Lord," as a sort of afterthought while walking home from the school.

Have we prayed fervently for our husbands, asking God to bless their day, guard their spirits in the turmoil of the work world, and be their strength and shield, using them for His glory? I didn't, not until after he was retired. And when I finally got around to it, the Holy Spirit used the occasion to give my spirit a wakeup call. I was praying fervently for John, and had been for a whole two or three minutes, and was about to wrap up by saying, "And Lord, if there is anything in me that is an impediment to him, show it to me so that I can work on it." I often pray aloud when I'm out on my porch in the summer. It helps focus my scattered brain. I had gotten out the part about "if there is anything in me" when my loving Father whispered softly in my ear, "Did you say *if?*"

Have we prayed faithfully and consistently for our schools, our pastors, and our government leaders? Well, I'm going to risk having you picket the Christian bookstores shouting, "Get this slacker away from the typewriter!" and admit that I have not. Not consistently.

None of this is being loyal to God. He created us for communion with Him. He came every evening to the Garden to walk with Adam and Eve and hear about their day. How different would this poor, old world be today if either one of them had held up their hand and said, "Slow down there. You may well be right, serpent old boy, but I think I'll check this out with the Big Guy before I go any further."

God wants to impart wisdom to us. He wants to comfort us. He wants to guide our steps. Proverbs 3:6 says, "Trust in the Lord with all of your heart and lean not upon your own understandings. Acknowledge him in all your ways, and he will direct your path." How do you acknowledge Him in all your ways? One of the biggies is by stopping to talk to Him about it all.

C. S. Lewis talked about how we so often feel like fish out of water, how time seems unfathomable somehow. People say things like, "How did you get so big? It seems like just yesterday you were in an infant seat." The reason Lewis gives for this is that we were not created for this fallen world where time is a measurable thing. We were created for eternity. That seems absolutely on target to me.

In the light of that, it occurred to me that when we pray, we really are "calling home" from far away, asking advice on how to cope with a totally foreign experience. We need to be loyal to the God who created us by reading the letters He has written us, by following the advice they contain, and by calling home with consistent prayer. John Bunyon defined prayer this way:

> Prayer is the sincere, sensible, affectionate pouring out of the heart or soul to God, through Christ, in the strength and assistance of the Holy Spirit, for such things as God has promised, or according to the Word of God, for the good of the church, with submission in faith to the will of God.[7]

That quote is printed again at the end of the chapter, right before the discussion questions. I advise reading it over a few times a week until you start to understand all the parts of it. Better yet, get his little book, *Praying In the Spirit* and study it either alone or with a friend. Remember, Bunyon wrote in the mid-1600s, and he's still in print! He must have been on to something.

What To Abandon

Finally, I want to add a post-script by talking about what you should not be loyal to. There may be things in your heritage that are not godly: profanity, prejudice, the attitudes and demands of an ungodly parent, and the demands of an ungodly government.

Back to Bonhoeffer: Focus on the Family[8] has a great radio drama production about his life. If you are unfamiliar with his story, I urge you to get it. Let your older kids listen to it. Just knowing about the man's life will pull you a little higher up the mountain in understanding of what it takes to follow our Lord.

The point of returning to Bonhoefer is that while it is incumbent on us to be loyal to our country that obligation ends when the country demands ungodly things of us.

In America, we are fortunate that, while our government sometimes allows ungodly things, it has not yet started *requiring* us to take part in them. You can homeschool your kids if you don't like what the public schools are teaching. If you are a healthcare worker, you can refuse to participate in abortions, although you may have to go to court to do it without losing your job. If the time comes when the government does require participation in ungodly activities, pray that we will all have the courage of Bonhoefer.

The story of Jonathan, the son of King Saul and best friend of young David, illustrates the companion point of not being loyal to the demands of an ungodly parent. Jonathan honored his father, Saul, so long as he could do so without betraying his own conscience, but when he knew his father was plotting to kill his innocent friend, he knew to whom the higher loyalty was due. I think the part where he *did* honor him in all he could is important. The Bible doesn't excuse us from honoring wrong-minded parents, except where they are demanding *we* do wrong things.

We are excused from lying for them. We are not excused from speaking to them in a respectful tone of voice. We are excused from giving them money to gamble or get drunk with. We aren't excused from making sure their heating bill is paid. I'm sure you get the picture.

Wash It with Soap

Foul language is another thing many people either grew up hearing or got used to in high school or college. I told my son when he was in junior high that if he ever felt compelled by locker-room peer pressure to cuss a little, he should make sure he used good, clean (if vulgar), four-letter Anglo Saxon words referring to body function but to make sure he never used the name of God in those situations. And those Anglo Saxon words were only for locker room situations, never at home, never in mixed company.

This flies in the face of current secular wisdom. There are many of those good, clean, four-letter Anglo Saxon words referring to body function that cannot be said on television where "Oh my God!" is common fare. Check the Bible. Taking the Lord's name in vain is one of the Big Ten. Striving to become cleaner and purer in thought and speech is part of the journey—a la Philippians 4:8.

In The Message, a portion of Colossians 1:3, reads, "It wasn't long ago that you were doing all that stuff and not knowing any better. But you know better now, so make sure it's all gone for good: bad temper, irritability, profanity, dirty talk."

If you have some bad habits in this area, I'd advise working on getting God's name un-trivialized first. When you have that down, start replacing those good, clean, Anglo Saxon words referring to body function with something more honorable, pure, lovely, and gracious.

Turn It Around

Some may have things in their upbringing that are harder to get rid of than a foul mouth. One of the most pernicious and absolutely abominable to God is racial prejudice. How much more clearly could He put it? "For as many of you as were baptized into Christ have put on Christ. There is neither Jew nor Greek, there is neither slave nor free, there is neither male nor female; for you are all one in Christ Jesus" (Galations 3:28). He has covered race, social status, and gender. We really have *no* grounds left for prejudice.

Haman was not born hating Jews. It was not built into his genetic code because he was a descendant of a King killed by the Israelites. He was taught to hate. We can also be taught not to hate.

I would like to tell you the story of a very wise and brave woman. She was raised in a southern family where prejudice was rife and the Civil War was not over, just on pause. Paradoxically, these were in most ways good, Bible-believing people who helped their neighbors and who were honest and just, but they had one glaring defect in their moral character. Somehow, during the course of her young adulthood, it became clear to the woman that it was indeed a defect. She thought to herself, "I think it is too late for me. I can change the way I act, but I can't change the way I feel. It's not too late for my children though. I will *not* bring them up with these wrong attitudes."

So she went to work, making sure her own and her husband's tongues were under control. She taught her child that you should never judge people on appearances of any kind but on the way they acted—on their character. She made sure her child had a chance to play with children from a lot of different backgrounds. And she succeeded. Her child did not have the destructive prejudices she herself had grown up with.

When she was an old woman, she had a stroke, and somehow, after a stroke, your mind falls back into the patterns of speech you first learned as a child. The first name to her lips when she tried to talk to someone was always her older sister's. When she woke in the night needing something, she said, "Mama?"

And when she saw a black person on television or walking down the street, she called them "dark-ies." Her daughter was appalled. How could this be? Slowly, it became clear to her what her mother had done. And she knew that without this late-life afflic-tion she would never really have had the measure of how brave and determined and never-ending a battle her mother had fought to give her this great gift. I know this is a true story, because she was my mother.

Do not honor prejudice of any kind in your upbringing. With the help of God, you can turn it around in one generation.

In Psalm 48, one of the sons of Korah wrote about looking up to Jerusalem, about thinking on what God had done, about learning His ways; and the reason given for doing it all is in verse 13: "That you may tell the next generation that He is God."

One of the ways to do that is to let them see you being loyal to Him, to your country, and to them by learning His ways, following His ways, and praying.

Prayer is the sincere, sensible, affectionate
pouring out of the heart or soul to God,
through Christ,
in the strength and assistance of the Holy Spirit
for such things as God has promised,
or according to the Word of God,
for the good of the church
with submission in faith to the will of God.

—John Bunyan, Bedford Prison
1662

DISCUSSION QUESTIONS

1. In general terms, without gossiping, how have you seen a breakdown of family loyalty in our society?

   _____

   _____

   _____

   _____

2. Did you vote in the last election? Why or why not? Do you agree or disagree with the author's assessment of the importance of voting?

   _____

   _____

   _____

   _____

3. How often do you 'call home'?

   _____

   _____

   _____

   _____

4. Which area of loyalty to God do you have the most trouble with?

    a. Consistently reading God's Word
    b. Acting on what God has shown you
    c. Praying fervently and often

_____

_____

_____

_____

5. Share with each other any victories you've had in these areas.

_____

_____

_____

_____

6. Think about and share (or not) what things from your upbringing you want to pass on or not pass on.

_____

_____

_____

_____

CHAPTER 3

Documentation and Attention to Detail

The subject of this chapter is so mundane, so connected to the nuts and bolts of life, it seemed a caution was in order. These studies *are* very nitty-gritty, they are "this-world" oriented. I don't want anybody to go away with the idea that these how-to-live-wisely lessons I've worked up by looking at the Book of Esther have anything to do with salvation. That comes only, always and forever, by trusting in the finished work of Jesus Christ.

These lessons deal with learning how to live in this fallen world within the context of that salvation. They are about what Jesus would have us do, about using this gift of life in a way that honors Him. You may be wondering, "How does documentation and attention to detail have anything to do with honoring God?"

This was one of the surprises God popped on me while studying Esther. Bev and I were reading along, keeping a sharp eye out for points of wisdom for counselors, when we came to the night the king had insomnia. We were trying to spot how God had delivered the Jewish population of the Persian Empire. What specific earthly things had He used?

Had He used the prayers of the faithful? Yes. They were praying and fasting. He was listening. Had He strengthened someone to a great act of courage? He certainly had; Esther went right into totally forbidden territory, risking the king's wrath and her own life.

These things were important. They were the foundation on which deliverance was built, but what was the lynchpin? What turned it around? It was at the point where God disrupted the king's sleep and he decided that a little dull reading of the official chronicles might lull him off that the tide turned. And it all hung on the fact that someone had kept careful records.

The story of the murder plot and who had saved the king's life by warning him of it caused him to wonder if that man had ever been rewarded. Since the man was Mordecai, that was the beginning of the end for Haman. He had just finished building a gallows on which he planned to hang Mordecai, when the events of Esther 6:1–10 intervened. The record of Mordecai's loyalty saved him and doomed Haman.

Once I saw that careful record keeping was involved, other biblical examples sprang readily to mind. Right there in Esther 4:8 we are shown that Mordecai himself was careful to document exactly what the king had ordered before he asked Esther to risk her life trying to do something about it. He didn't say, "Hey, I hear the king has a big pogrom planned." No! He sent her a copy of the decree.

Later, in the Bible, after some of the exiles had returned to try to rebuild Jerusalem and the Persian authorities tried to tell Ezra that he had no legal right to be there, he was able to say 'check the records'. He appealed to the current king who checked, and, sure enough, there was Darius' decree.

Maintaining Order

In a civilized society, one of the ways order is maintained is through careful record keeping. Aggravated as we may get at some of the silly red tape that occasionally takes the place of carefully kept records, there are many instances where most of us would agree that we need *more* checking of the facts. Like these:

"OK, ...three convictions for grand larceny; 'fraid we can't use you in airport security, Ms. Smith."

"Let's see here, ...five indictments for child abuse, and you want to be an aide in my daycare center.... I don't think so!"

"Mmmmm, so I see here on the MVA computer link that your license was suspended twice in the last five years for drunk driving. Perhaps you should consider applying for a job as something other than a school bus driver, Mr. Jones."

I'm not advocating a "big brother" society where the privacy of our homes is invaded, our mail read, and our financial records monitored; but history, which basically involves the public actions of individuals, needs to be recorded. Not just the bad actions that must be recorded for public protection but also the praiseworthy actions, which can inspire others. This documented history serves to distinguish truth from lies.

Let's assume you decide to go into public service. As Mordecai found out, being in a trusted government position can start a lot of people looking at you. The position doesn't have to be as lofty as Mordecai's. The same principle applies to the president of the PTA and the Sunday school teacher. If there is anything rusty or tarnished in your life up to that point, you had better set it right out there on the table and do a little show and tell. If you don't, somebody else will search out the records and do it for you, to your much greater detriment.

On the other hand, if those who find your very existence irritating try to start tales about you that aren't true, like, "she was dishonorably discharged," it's useful to able to pull out the papers and prove them wrong.

Pssst...Did You Hear?

There is a sidelight that seems to fit here. Gossip is *usually* the transference of undocumented information. "Well, I heard that she told him ..." But, what if it *is* documented? (You *saw* the pregnancy test; you *were* the Sunday school teacher who got cussed out by the "crazy mom;" you were *watching* out the nursery room window when the preacher's kid kicked that other boy; and how about this one, you *have been* the personal recipient of all the gossip that Jane Doe passes on, and "she really needs to clean up her act, OK?")

Even if you have the documentation, unless the person you're telling is in a position of authority (you may, for instance need to tell the pastor's wife about what her son did), or in a position to help (it might be wise to tell the Sunday school superintendent about the "crazy mom"), then it's gossip.

Unless one of those two criteria is met, you need to keep it to yourself.

Here's a word of what? Encouragement? You *may* find it encouraging to know that two old warriors are battling on, or you may find it *dis*couraging to hear that it is possible to fight so long without total victory. Anyway, after thirty years of friendship and praying together, both of us fighting the temptation to gossip, a few years ago my dear friend, Dorothea, and I were simultaneously drawn to buy (each for the other one) a sweatshirt that read, "Dear Lord, please keep your arm around my shoulder and your hand over my mouth."

It's like exercising. You don't develop muscles by deciding to exercise but by actually doing it. Even then, you won't turn into Arnold overnight. But *nothing* will happen if you don't start. I want to encourage you to work your jaw muscles by letting the Lord help you close your mouth before the gossip comes out.

If you have any doubts about the seriousness of this offense, just check out I Corinthians 6:9b–11: "Do not be deceived; neither the immoral, nor idolaters, nor adulterers, nor homosexuals, nor thieves, nor the greedy, nor drunkards, nor revilers" (translation: gossips), "nor robbers will inherit the kingdom of God. And such were some of you."

And such were *all* of us. In God's eyes, it's pretty notorious company we gossips keep. The fact that we safely trust in the righteous blood of Jesus to save us and not in our filthy rags of deeds doesn't excuse us from working with God to clean up those deeds. Remember, undocumented information passed along is gossip, and documented information passed along to people who have no legitimate need to know is also gossip.

Write It Down

Many of the statements from Henry Blackaby's great study, *Experiencing God*, will never leave me. One of them is, "If the God of the universe tells you something, write it down"[1].

I think journaling is one of the most productive disciplines a Christian can cultivate, but I was a long time coming to it. That seems odd, since I am a person to whom writing comes easily. In grade school I kept diaries. If you come across one of them, remember, I led a rich fantasy life.

In junior high and high school, I churned out reams of very bad poetry. In college I wrote obscure, irreverent short stories. As a young mother, I returned to poetry. It wasn't great, but it wasn't quite as bad as the earlier stuff. Here's a short one some of you may identify with.

I don't know how
To reconcile my life
To be a mother and
a lover and a wife
and not lose me:
the girl who writes all night
and sings in trees

Then, as I started growing a bigger garden, canning more, sewing more, leading Girl Scouts, learning to cook, running to soccer, ballet, and football, writing became a victim of my overstuffed calendar.

I know God was speaking to me through those years, because looking back, I can see that I was growing. I was hearing good preaching every Sunday, learning from excellent Bible study teachers, reading classic Christian books, and even doing a few independent studies. I did the study I referred to in the last chapter, the one on balance.

The reason I only had one example to share from it was because that's all I remember. I didn't write any of it down! All that study, and all I've got to show are the general conclusions I came to and one example. Don't make that mistake. Remember, "If the Lord of the universe tells you something, write it down."

Everybody journals differently. The journals I started about eight years ago, the first time my small group did the *Experiencing God* study—you know, the one where I learned "if the Lord of the universe tells you something, write it down"—are full of everything from the trivial and mundane to notes on the study that I wanted to share with my small group. "It will be very hot today and still no rain." "A good insight today, while doing *Experiencing God*. The question was, 'How have you been responding to God's leading?' My answer was, 'foot-dragging.' Then it dawned on me that that is exactly what an obedient child does. 'Yes, Mama, I'm coming.' And she really is but very slowly with a lot of distractions. I've been praying that I would be like an obedient child. I need to change that to a willing and eager child."

Would you believe it? There was even more poetry. Here's one you might get a kick out of.

The natural tendency,
never mastered, just subdued,
is to let the ragged tatters—
bits and pieces falling off—
lie where they fall.
The bed, unmade and unremembered,
Half-read magazines beside the chair,
weeds pulled and left to die upon the grass,
seem small held up against Amazing Grace.
But that sweet sound is savored best
astride the humpback camel of obedience.

I would tell more,
but I must go and make the bed.

What Good Is It?

It really doesn't matter what you write, what you write it in, or if you write every day. It's not a diary, it's a journal, so just start and keep it handy. Let the Spirit lead you. You cannot possibly know how God will use the wandering thoughts, details of your day, or the well-thought-out insights you record. You cannot know how God will use any of your obedient acts.

God may use your journaling efforts to bless you as you reread them in months or years to come. My daughter-in-law, Kelly, kept a detailed prayer journal when she was in college. One of her prayers had been for a sign of spiritual growth in her parents. Then in the rush of the working world, getting married, and having babies, she lost track of her journal. When she came across it years later at a moment of despair and doubt, she was immensely blessed when she realized that the prayer had been answered. Her parents were now leading a small group Bible study in their home.

God may use it to bless others in your lifetime as you are able to recapture the insights He gave you and pass them along. My friend Marilyn Anderes felt called to "dwell" in one area of Scripture for a whole year. So everything she thought about went down in a special journal. Everything she read on that topic went into the journal with the reference. Every scripture God showed her that seemed to throw light on the area where she was dwelling went into the journal. Every retreat and Bible study she has ever led has been based on those journals. She has a big stack of them now. Each one is on a different topic. If she has a new insight on "Come Higher, There's More," she can go to the journal that is just for that topic and add it.

People keep prayer journals, topical journals, stream-of-consciousness journals, and multi-purpose, multi-dimensional journals, like mine. There is no one right way. You can make up a style that will suit *you*. God may use it to bless you, as He did Kelly. He may use it to bless others, as He has used Marilyn's, or He may use it in ways you can't even imagine after you have long been home with Him. This is the first entry in my first journal: "With my heart in my hand, along with my pen, I begin this journal on April 26, 1997 and pray that I will be given perseverance and memory to continue it faithfully, for the Lord has long been calling me to it, and I have long been planting my feet like a stubborn mule and not doing it. I am finally inspired today by reading some of the journaled words of Cotton Mather, written in 1695, and preserved these 300+

years for the edification of those who will find the time to read them."

Mr. Mather could not have imagined the world we live in, let alone that his words would be used by God to inspire a harried housewife/market gardener.

Our pastor once preached a whole sermon taken mainly from the journals of John Wesley. I'm sure that's not one of the things John Wesley imagined might come about as a result of his jotting down that he rose at five for study on a given morning.

The journals of John Quincy Adams have also been an inspiration to me. Reading the account of the details of his day gives me a higher standard to aim toward in the productive use of my time. Peter Marshall and John Manuel say this about him in *Sounding Forth the Trumpet*.

> In the tradition of his Puritan forefathers, he held himself accountable daily before God, recording in his journal those places where he was convicted of falling short of the mark. He has been called the Last Puritan, and he was indeed one of the last of that vanishing breed for whom obedience to God was the sole criterion for a life well lived.[2]

Because he kept his journals we have the example of that life well lived. History records people's public deeds. In a journal you can record your heart.

Right now, you may hardly be able to wait to put down this book and run to the store so you can pick up a notebook and start journaling. Or maybe you're itching to dig out the one you already started and haven't seen in a year or so. Or you may be thinking, "But writing *isn't* easy for me." Don't be intimidated. You don't have to write the great American novel. My first black, marbleized cover journal, (the kind you buy for school), took four years to fill. A similar one may last you ten years or the rest of your life.

Where I would spin a story, you may jot down some thing like:

Experiencing God, pg. 97
Obedient children—foot-dragging
Prayer—to be a willing and eager child

It will still remind you of the God-given insight and will still convey that insight to others.

God Sets the Example

God told Moses to write everything down in the book and also to speak it in the ear of Aaron. God's Holy Ghost writers always nail their narratives firmly into secular history. The writer of Esther, thought to be either Ezra or Mordecai himself, placed his story carefully by telling who was king and what city they were in. He also gave some hard genealogical facts. In chapter five, verses five and six, he told us exactly who Mordecai was back three generations, what tribe they were from, and that it was his great-grandpa who had been carried away captive from Jerusalem. He also told us that Haman was an Agagite and who his dad was. You'll remember that the very fact of his being an Agagite went a long way toward explaining his hatred for Jews.

Remember in grade school, if you were asked to write a five-hundred-word paper, how you'd count every word, adding a lot of extraneous detail and multiple adjectives to increase the count? Well, I don't think *this* stuff is just stuck in as ruffles and flourishes. Every bit of it was important to prove to the reader that he was reading history not a fable.

While the Bible specifically warns us against wasting time on "endless genealogies," it also sets an example of the importance of knowing who you are and where you come from. Here we are back at balance. Nehemiah took up a lot of space telling exactly who had come back to Jerusalem with him. Those biblical genealogies were necessary so that when the time came it could be shown that Jesus was descended from David, as prophesied. Here's the balance to be sought: while we are not to waste our precious time on endless genealogies, we are not to forget the stories of the past. We can use them as a foundation for building the future.

Keep the Stories Alive

Keeping family history—the stories of bravery, courage, faith, and even failure, mistakes, and laughter is one way of carrying out the commandment to "honor your father and your mother." This keeping of the family stories is another form of documentation. It says in Deuteronomy 4:9, "Only take heed, and keep your soul diligently, lest you forget the things which your eyes have seen, and lest they depart from your heart all the days of your life; make them known to your children, and your children's children."

When my dad died, I realized that since both he and I had been an only child, I was now the sole person who could tell his stories, and I started trying to get them down on paper. It would still have mattered, even if I hadn't had children to pass these stories to. My job was to record them. Figuring out how to use them was up to God.

Two of my favorite stories concern my great-grandfather. He was a tall, good-looking Irishman. According to his obituary, he was a wonderful storyteller and stirring speechmaker, who served several terms in Congress. That's just background to get the full flavor of the stories. Both take place at a large exposition around 1900 to which he took his three teenage daughters, one of whom was my grandmother. As they entered the fairgrounds, he put on his tall black silk top hat. "See this hat, girls?"

"Yes, Papa."

"Follow it!" And he walked away without looking back.

This is a story about leadership. Don't be so interested in whether anybody's following that you fail to keep your eye on the road ahead.

Later in the day, they came to a place selling that wondrous new invention, ice cream.

"Girls?"

"Yes, Papa"

"Would you like to have some ice cream?"

Hoping not to be thought demanding or impolite, the girls simpered, "We don't care, Papa." After a dramatic pause, he replied, "Well, neither do I," and they got no ice cream.

This story was told to me as an admonition to make a decision and boldly speak my honest opinion. It sunk in. Children learn best from stories. Nobody has ever accused me of not being able to make a decision. Sometimes it's the wrong one, but I make it and move on. I don't want to dither around and miss out on the ice cream.

These kinds of stories are more than lessons on living. They honor the memories of those who have gone before, and they make history come alive. Recording these things is more than "endless genealogies."

Into the seemingly endless genealogy of 1 Chronicles, chapter four, is stuck the three-sentence story of Jabez. All these millennia later, Bruce Wilkerson pulled some principles of Christian prayer from that story with which he has managed to reach an incredible number of people. His little book, *The Prayer of Jabez*[3], was on the secular bestseller list for at least a year. It can be truthfully argued that many people in the secular world have totally misunderstood his book and are using the prayer of Jabez as a sort of "magic incantation," but it is also true that many people who have never read any other book on prayer have been moved to pray and to seek God. Some may eventually be saved because of it. All of that was possible because some genealogist paused in his endless listings long enough to tell a story from someone's life.

Where to Start

There are all kinds of ways to tell your family stories. Perhaps the simplest is to get a loose-leaf notebook and draw a family tree on the first page, then tell the stories on subsequent pages. This will keep it clear in the minds of future generations who these people were and how they fit in to the family.

A photo album—the scrapbook kind, which gives you the option of writing on the pages is another good option. That way you have all the family pictures identified and the stories of what kind of people they were, right there by the picture. I did an album like that for my daughter as a Christmas present a few years ago. I made copies of all the family photos I could identify and then told their stories on the opposite page.

If, as was discussed earlier, a pen in your hand pretty much guarantees brain paralysis, you can talk into a tape recorder. You can get the people who are still around to talk into the tape recorder, or you can set up a video camera and do an interview. If the camera is mounted on an end table or tri-pod, you will be surprised how quickly everyone loosens up, and forgets the camera.

When Did She Get that Tetanus Shot?

It behooves us as women to look well to the ways of our households. (That's actually from Proverbs 31, one of the more aggravating books of the Bible, but I always feel like I'm quoting Janet Parshall[4] when I say it.) I happen to have married a GAO investigative auditor and have learned a lot from him about the importance of maintaining orderly records. Receipts, warrantees, school records, immunizations—you've got to keep track of this stuff!

People without the knack of record keeping can buy a file box or a pretty covered box of some sort and at least acquire the habit of stuffing everything into it. If it's all in one place, you can stir it with a stick until the bit you need rises to the surface. Clean it out every five years whether it needs it or not. Differently gifted people will come up with more methodical systems.

Attention To Detail

I saw a funny thing once while watching the Academy of Country Music Awards. Vince Gill said, "Twelve years ago, Garth Brooks exploded." He paused, looking smugly at the audience, then did a double take and said, "I'm sorry. There's no period there. Twelve years ago Garth Brooks exploded onto the country music scene."

It reminded me of a fourth-grade lesson on the importance of punctuation and how it can change the meaning of a sentence. There was also one on words that sound alike and how spelling them correctly makes a difference. The sentence, "I saw too," depending on the spelling, can mean, "You are correct, I also saw that." Or it can mean, "You are mistaken, there was not one. I clearly saw a pair of them." This is where we shift from record keeping to attention to detail.

Although "Veggie Tales" shows her serving "McFood," I'm pretty sure that when Esther invited Aheseurus and Haman to her banquet she paid a lot of attention to detail. I'll bet the servants were drilled in proper presentation, the flowers were fresh, there were no spots on the linen, the hot food was hot, and the cold food was cold. Esther herself was undoubtedly a model of impeccable grooming. Her spirit was innocent as a dove (she was trying to serve God and save her people), but her mind was wise as a serpent. She was putting the king in a receptive mood.

And what about God's incredible attention to detail? Remember how He disturbed the king's sleep and the king had the records read in hope it would lull him back to the Land of Nod? At the exact moment when the king started wondering how he could honor Mordecai, in waltzed Haman, the very man to ask. Old Haman thought *he* would be the one getting the goodies, so he laid it on pretty thick and then had to serve it up for Mordecai.

God's detailed timing came into play later in the story, too. In Esther 7:2–8, we read that at the exact moment when Haman was begging for mercy and throwing himself, literally, on the mercy of the queen, the king returned and thought he was seeking considerably more than mercy there in the queen's lap.

God's Detailed Creation

Attention to detail is one of the things God has demonstrated before us in creation. The more scientists learn about the world, the more apparent that becomes.

Romans 1:20 has always said, "Ever since the creation of the world his invisible nature, namely his eternal power and deity, has been clearly perceived in the things that have been made. So they are without excuse." For thousands of years people found that to be true. The marvel of creation was always one of the strongest arguments for the existence of God.

Then along came Charles Darwin who made some perfectly logical assumptions based on then current knowledge and his own limited observations. That's what a theory is, a working hypothesis about what you will find as you investigate further. At that time, little was known about cell structure, and DNA hadn't even been discovered. The amoeba was thought to be a simple blob of unspecialized plasma. The science of statistics was in its infancy.

Darwin himself said that if his theory was correct the fossil evidence would show up to prove it. Well, here we are, all these many years later, and the fossil evidence has done exactly the opposite. It doesn't show slow change over long periods of time but sudden explosions of life forms with huge gaps between them.

God's attention to detail was so magnificently complete that, in this day and age with its electron microscopes and computers to crunch massive numerical analyses, we have, with the unraveling of the genetic code, the proof that no hunk of plasma can possibly be described as simple. We also have the statistical proof that infinite time plus infinite chance could not have resulted in the development of even one species of fish, let alone the rich diversity of life on this planet.

Many cutting edge scientists now acknowledge the necessity for an intelligent creative force. Consider this analogy made by a prominent statistician: He said that a living organism emerging spontaneously from the primordial soup is about as likely as that "a tornado sweeping through a junkyard might assemble a Boeing 747 from the materials there-in."

Darwin himself said that the most telling argument against his theory was the sparsity of the fossil record. He was quite sure that would be remedied in time. Yet no less an expert than Colin Patterson, senior paleontologist at the British Museum of Natural History (home of the world's largest fossil collection), when queried on having not included any evolutionary transitional fossils in his book, *Evolution*, said this: "If I knew of any, fossil or living, I would certainly have included them"[5].

If you need more ammunition with which to battle for the minds of your children, your friends, or maybe even your own mind, you can start with the three sources I have listed in the bibliography. They are Philip Johnson's *Darwin on Trial*, Chuck Colson's *How Now Shall We Live?*, and David T. Moore's great series of sermons entitled *Somebody's Trying to Make a Monkey out of You.*

Yet the lower echelons of academia still seem glued to the theory of evolution. Your children will still find it taught as gospel in the public elementary and secondary schools. It is basic to all undergraduate college curricula and in postgraduate liberal arts fields.

Why is that? In every other area of science everyone wants to be in the vanguard. We want our cell phones to give us stock quotes, instant messages, and take and transmit pictures. We feel we really need the latest generation of computers or our Internet connections are just too slow. If we're sick, we want the latest and most promising treatment. So why has academia been living in denial of the death of the theory of evolution?

Well, think about it. If we are just highly evolved blobs of plasma, then there is no Higher Power, no Creator, to whom we might owe some debt of allegiance. There are no absolutes and no rules to follow that cannot be changed to suit the situation. The whole postmodern construct is based on that assumption. Or should I say, the postmodern *de*construct? Topple Darwinism and the whole philosophical house of cards that has been built on it will tumble, taking with it the people who have based their lives and their careers on it's validity. Regardless of how many people insist on worshipping in front of the sarcophagus, Darwinism has been killed. How? By God's wonderful attention to detail.

What's It Look Like?

I needed some good examples of the importance of attention to detail in daily life, so I thought I would have to go to my friends for help. "I am not," I thought to myself, "the poster child for attention to detail." When I knit or crochet a baby blanket, it usually gets wrapped and presented without the painstaking addition of a delicate edging. I clean house in a general way, not worrying too much about the corners or under the couch. In my gardening, a bit of semantic "fluff" (changing the word "weed" to "native plant species") covers a multitude of lack of attention to detail.

I was actually writing the first part of this, confessing my failure as a detail-oriented person, when

I was shown that God does enable me to pay attention to details in the areas where He has called me to serve. When I write a lesson like this or a poem, I go over and over it, polishing, making sure I've been clear, that I've gotten the grammar right, and that the funny bits aren't all at the beginning or the end.

It seems clear now that even if you aren't naturally a person who even *sees* the details that need tending to, you should be looking for God to strengthen you in that way in the endeavors where you are gifted to serve. Be sure not to limit Him in your mind. You can't, of course, actually limit Him, but you can limit your own ability to think about Him and relate to Him.

Many years ago (probably thirty), a group of women were working after Bible study to clean up the old church kitchen. Someone described her salvation experience. I jumped right in and said, "No, …it's more like …blah, blah, blah." A few minutes later, as we worked alone together in another part of the kitchen, our pastor's wife said to me, very quietly, "You know, Penny, we have to allow God the freedom to work differently in different people."

Whoa! I don't think I ever told her what an impact that simple statement had on me. It opened up a whole new way of thinking for me. It took me out of the middle of every picture. It eventually worked on my heart to expand my vision of God from the child's "Yes, Jesus loves me, the Bible tells me so," to an ever expanding vision of the magnitude of God which resulted in a paean of praise more comparable to a Bach Mass.

That paves the way for saying never doubt that God will take care of the details. If He doesn't strengthen *you* to do it, He may send alongside you someone who is uniquely gifted for administration and detail. One summer, my friend, Nancy Schrumm, pulled together a group of mentors to do a program she called WOW. The Lord had moved Nancy and me separately and in different ways to pray about starting this program. We have seen evidence that a lot of people were blessed by it, both mentors and participants, so we're pretty sure we were doing what God wanted us to do.

But frankly, done in our own strength, it could have been a disaster. I have already confessed my failings in the sphere of attention to detail, and while she is devoted to "excellence," Nancy is a big-picture person. So what did God do? In His wisdom, He did not strengthen either of us to handle the adminis-trative details. We were each carrying a full load, doing other things He had called us to. What He did was send us Heather Kilpatrick, a sort of genius of managerial skills.

Don't expect God to strengthen you to do it all. He may differently with different people, remember, or He may bring together a *body* of believers, differently gifted, none able to do it alone, who can work together to accomplish the mission He's sent you on.

Details Are Important

God laid down incredibly detailed plans for Noah to follow in building the Ark. I'm pretty sure that could have gone badly awry if Noah had decided to add his own little bright ideas to God's perfect plans for a boat that would carry the weight, stand up to the rough seas, and stay afloat.

God also paid immaculate attention to detail in prophecy. One of the many ways we know that Jesus is who He said He was is that ten or twelve other people, some hundreds and some thousands of years before he was born, told us exactly how it was all going to happen. Statistics again. The likelihood of *all* those prophecies falling accidentally into place in the circumstances of one lifetime is nil.

It was in reading a book about Old Testament prophecy that I first had the mind-bending revelation, "Oh my, He's really there!" As Daniel told the king of Persia, "There is a God in heaven who reveals mysteries" (Daniel 2:28).

Strive to be obedient. If the Lord of the universe tells you something, write it down. Pay attention to the details, even if you aren't the one handling them. Watch to see how God will put them together. Second Chronicles 16:9 says, "For the eyes of the Lord run to and fro throughout the whole earth, to show his might in behalf of those whose heart is blameless toward him."

DISCUSSION QUESTIONS

1. Has there ever been a time when the fact that something was documented made a difference in your life?

   _____

   _____

   _____

   _____

2. Do you keep a journal? If not, will you now think about starting one? If yes, share what the rewards have been.

   _____

   _____

   _____

   _____

3. Are you a detail person or a broad-strokes person? What are the advantages and disadvantages of your personality type? Have you seen God putting people with the opposite style into your life just when you needed them?

   _____

   _____

   _____

   _____

4. Do you have a plan for teaching your kids (or grandkids or nieces and nephews) cutting-edge science to counterbalance what they will get in school? Share some ways you could do that.

_____

_____

_____

_____

5. Have you gossiped or listened to gossip? (Hint: the only honest answer is yes.)

_____

_____

_____

_____

6. Share strategies for overcoming that sin.

_____

_____

_____

_____

7. Do you have any family stories, old or new, that should be recorded for future generations?

_____

_____

_____

_____

CHAPTER 4

LEADING BY EXAMPLE

One thing my friend and I found as we studied Esther was that a lot of Mordecai's lessons were taught not by word but by example. That seemed to make them widely applicable and was the genesis of this book. After all, as our mamas taught us, "Actions speak louder than words."

Esther saw Mordecai doing a lot of brave and right-on things. We are never told whether he also taught her the principles behind his actions, but we know she was able to learn by watching him. She saw him praying and fasting, standing firm in his faith, displaying great courage by refusing to bow to Haman, practicing family loyalty in his care of her, showing faithfulness in his execution of that loyalty, and finally, demonstrating his trust in God to work it all out if they prayed and did their best.

In marriage, parenting, friendship, mentoring, and leadership—which can range from CEO to mother—people are looking not only at what we say but also at what we do and how we do it.

The ways in which we handle our daily tasks (whether imparting the principles of honesty to a four-year-old, dealing with difficult employees, or doing the bookkeeping for a home-based business) tells people who we are, how we think, and what's important to us.

I was a Girl Scout leader in my mist-shrouded youth. I always tried to lead by example. "Of course, you can learn to carve with a pocket knife. Just remember to keep your whole hand around the handle. Don't put your thumb on the …ouch! …blade, see? Don't put your thumb on the blade!"

I think the most remembered instance of my leading by example (we had a reunion one summer, and believe me, they all remembered) was on a camping trip when we took one last hike to practice newly acquired orienteering skills. Each patrol followed a different set of written directions to a distant location using their compasses, landmarks, and stepped-off measurements. They had just reassembled at the hilltop starting point where I was waiting. As I started to lead them down the hill, they spotted their parents' cars arriving in the valley and started to run. In my stentorian Girl Scout leader voice, I shouted, "Halt! Now! Never run downhill! It's dangerous!" I then proceeded to run down the hill to get back in the front of the line, fell, and broke my foot. There are all kinds of leading by example. In this study I will attempt to concentrate on leading by setting a *good* example.

Henry Blackaby said, "What you do reveals what you think about God, regardless of what you say"[1]. Chuck Colson told a story that illustrates this.

> There cannot be any more sacred or humbling trust for any human being than to go forth saying, "I am a Christian." I remember one particular day some years ago, standing in line at the Jakarta airport. I was very tired. I had flown all night, and then I got held up at immigration. We had a very busy schedule that day. The people who were supposed to have escorted us through customs, didn't. To make a long story short, I was feeling very frustrated, standing there in line for half an hour....
>
> Well, two years later I received a letter from a lawyer of Chinese descent in Singapore. "Dear Mr. Colson," he wrote, "I grew up in the superstitions of the Chinese people. I had no interest in Christianity, but I sent my son and daughter to a Sunday school, because I

wanted them to learn some moral teachings. A missionary came to the church one day when I was delivering the kids. He held up your book, *Born Again*, and said something about you. I was fascinated by that, and went and got the book. I didn't read it, but the cover was on my table at home."

"Two years ago (you wouldn't remember this), I was standing in the immigration line in Jakarta, and I looked over and saw your profile, which was on the book. I watched you for the next half hour. I was tired and frustrated and angry, but you weren't. (If he had only known.) I went home; I got that book; I read it; and in the end, in tears, I gave my life to Christ."

You never know! You never know how God will use a casual, positive word, a smile to someone who is discouraged, a helping hand to somebody who needs it, an act of faithfulness to what you say you believe, a determination not to let the carnal self get the better of you. You may never know how God will use that.[2]

Consider also what Eugene Peterson says in his introduction to the Book of Philemon, in The Message:

Every movement we make in response to God has a ripple effect, touching family, neighbors, friends, community. Belief in God alters our language. Love of God affects our daily relationships. Hope in God enters into our work. Also their opposites—unbelief, indifference and despair. None of these movements and responses, beliefs and prayers, gestures and searches, can be confined to the soul. They spill out and make history. If they don't, they are under suspicion of being fantasies at best, hypocrisies at worst.

Just as you may never know who will ultimately be blessed by your journaling, the unseen effect on other people of just watching how you live can be great.

We see in Esther 3:2–6 that Mordecai did a very simple thing. He did not bow down to Haman. The effects of that were very far reaching, and we have talked about the fact that it's important to do what's right just because it's right and not in anticipation of the possible consequences. We also said that lot of what ensued after Mordecai refused to bow down to Haman was short-term disaster, but the long-term and the internal results of practicing righteousness are always good.

Who is Looking?

I want to push you into a paradigm shift. We've been looking at Mordecai's actions from inside the palace, but how about the view from the street? He was sitting in the gate. He could be seen from both sides. We're not told so, but doesn't it seem likely that many in the Jewish population of Susa were heartened and strengthened in their faith by what they saw Mordecai doing?

The fact that we aren't told is so typical of this aspect of the Christian life. It was a very special blessing for Mr. Colson to get that letter. Normally, we just don't know.

It's not like that great old movie, *It's a Wonderful Life*. Angels don't really need to earn their wings. They are not dead people trying to work their way up the heavenly corporate ladder. They are specially created beings, made just the way they are right from the beginning. When we're depressed, they don't walk us through our past to see what came about as a result of our obedience.

It *was* through obedience to biblical principles that all the fruitful results of George Bailey's life came about. He took care of his little brother, honored his father and his mother, worked hard, protected and defended an inebriated employer, and as a businessman he treated everyone in town with equal respect.

I think the reason the movie has continued to resonate with so many people is that (except for the angel part), it does reflect reality. God uses ordinary lives, lived in obedience to Him, to generate good things. That's reality. And the ordinary, obedient people living those lives seldom get more than a glimpse of any of it. That's reality too. You have to trust that He's using it.

What Will They Think?

The Message translation of Romans 12:1 explains it well. "So here's what I want you to do, God helping you. Take your everyday, ordinary life your sleeping, eating, going to work and walking around life—and place it before God as an offering." We're back to the statement that what you do reveals what you believe about God, regardless of what you say.

We know from John 17:20-23 and John 14:31 that the world will judge God by what it sees us doing. Francis of Assisi said, "Preach Jesus at all times, and if you must, use words."[3]

What we do and how we do it tells our children, our husbands, our friends, our acquaintances, our co-workers, and casual observers exactly what we believe. If all these people assume that as a Christian you are striving to be Christlike, would they decide from watching you that Jesus is patient and kind or cranky and short-tempered? Would they perceive that He is ultimate, unmovable righteousness or wishy-washy and "tolerant" in the worst sense of that recently much-misused word? Would they conclude He was compassionate or indifferent? Forgiving or judgmental?

Maybe you really believe God is love, and you know that Jesus told us in Matthew that if we don't forgive our enemies, God will not forgive us. But perhaps you've never had that bolt of lightening experience that makes you realize that these teachings are meant to impact the way you *live*.

At the end of the Sermon on the Mount, Jesus said, "Everyone then who hears these words of mine and does them will be like a wise man who built his house upon the rock; and the rain fell, and the floods came, and the winds blew and beat against that house, but it did not fall, because it had been founded on the rock. And everyone who hears these words of mine and does not do them will be like a foolish man who built his house upon the sand; and the rain fell, and the floods came, and the winds blew and beat against the house, and it fell; and great was the fall of it" (Mathew 7:24-27).

Here's what Eugene Peterson said in his introduction to the Book of Ephesians in the Message: "What we know about God and what we do for God have a way of getting broken apart in our lives. The moment the organic unity of faith and behavior is damaged in any way, we are incapable of living out the full humanity for which we were created." We break this organic unity all the time. We are really good at dichotomizing how we think about our faith from how we think about our everyday life.

A clear example of that is in the area of forgiveness. We know we are to forgive and pray for our enemies, so we work really hard at learning how to pray sincerely these kinds of prayers: "Lord, these terrorists are lost sheep. I do not ask you for mercy for them, but I do pray for their salvation. Father, I am not so Christlike that I can say, as I replay the collapse of the Trade Towers in my mind, 'Father forgive them, for they know not what they do.' But I *want* to be that Christlike, and I ask you to continue to work on my heart until I am."

We have no doubt that these people are our enemies. We can strive to leave the execution of justice to our government to whom God has given both the authority and the responsibility for that task. *Our* marching order is different: forgive! It may be hard to act on it, but at least we know what it is.

But the neighbor who borrows things that we never see again, the whining child who has just gotten on our last nerve, the "friend" who criticizes us behind our backs, or the family members who seem to think it is always their turn to take and ours to give, aren't our *enemies*, are they? They are just plain aggravating!

It is in these situations however, where the world will judge God by how it sees us acting. They'll never hear the fine things we manage to say to God in our quiet times (nor are they meant to), but they will notice if we scream after our sister's departing back, "Well, I *had* to do it myself, 'cause I knew for sure *you* wouldn't!"

They will notice if we call our nine-year-old a hopeless idiot while cruising the aisles of the supermarket. The kids will know we don't think of their dad as God's provision for us all and the strong head of the family if we belittle him and make jokes at his expense in their presence.

Paul was talking about fixing this disunity between belief and action when he said, "Make a clean break with all cutting, backbiting, profane talk. Be gentle with one another, sensitive. Forgive one another as quickly and thoroughly as God forgave you" (Ephesians 4:15, The Message).

Where Are You a Leader?

This area of forgiveness and gentle speech are part of the disunity between belief and action through which people will look at us and draw conclusions about God. There is more to it, though, than what we display publicly.

Probably, as women, the place where our "leading by example" has the most impact is as mothers, beloved aunts, grandmothers, and Sunday school teachers. The kids will ultimately do what they see us doing, and they will believe what we teach them by example. If they see us reading the Bible every day and they hear us citing Scripture verses as the basis for decisions, they will believe the Bible is important.

Here's an example. You are ironing. Your child, your grandchild, or the nephew you are watching wants you to come and play a game. I'm only going to give the mother's end of this conversation because you can easily imagine the child's end.

"In a few minutes, honey. Mommy wants to get all of Daddy's shirts ironed and in his closet...."

"That was good listening! Yes, at breakfast Daddy did only ask me to get one done for him, but you know, the Bible tells us to go the extra mile...."

"No, honey, it's not talking about exercise, it's talking about helping people. It means you should do more than you are asked to do, so the other person will be blessed. Think how happy Daddy will be to see all his shirts ironed and ready to wear...."

"No, I'm not done yet. I tell you what, why don't you sit down in here and we will play 'I spy' while I finish."

What has the child learned by what you did? That the Bible is a reliable guide for how to act. That making Daddy happy is important to Mommy. And that *he* is important to Mommy, because Mommy thought up a way to play with him, even while she was ironing.

Keeping It All Together

The Bible recommends leading by example to women in marriage too. James 3:1 says, "Likewise you wives, be submissive to your husbands, so that some, though they do not obey the word, may be won without a word by the behavior of their wives.". If your husband or your boss is not saved, what are the chances that he will see the light as a result of you preaching to him and scolding him? Right! But if he sees you handling the aggravations and frustrations of your day with patience, wisdom, and forgiveness, pouring yourself out in service, he just might decide you've got something he wants.

My longtime pastor, George Anderson, preached a great sermon a few years ago. He's preached a lot of great sermons, but the one I'm thinking about was called, "Being Who You Say You Are." One of the things he talked about was the definition of the word "integrity." The word describes a condition where all the parts of a machine, or all the aspects of a person, fit together to make a smoothly functioning whole. You have probably heard something like this said in news reports, "When the tail broke away, the integrity of the aircraft was compromised."

If you say you believe one thing but your actions portray a whole different worldview, your integrity has been compromised. Your parts are working against each other. No one is apt to want to buy a car if they can hear the gears grinding and the brakes squealing, and no one is going to be tempted to buy into Christianity if our mouths are saying *this* while our bodies are running off doing *that*!

Jesus said, "No man can serve two masters. Either he will love the one and hate the other, or he will be devoted to the one and despise the other. You cannot serve both God and Mammon" (Mathew 6:24). This is only one of the places in the Bible where we are taught that the love of money is the root of all evil, and we're all pretty familiar with the concept that prioritizing material wealth above God only leads to trouble. It disrupts our integrity.

I HAVE A RIGHT TO....

There is another form of unrighteous mammon in our American culture that Satan has grabbed onto and uses very effectively to disrupt the integrity of Christians. It is the concept that we have "rights."

Don't get me wrong. I am a great respecter of the US Constitution, and I think it is important to our nation that the Bill of Rights be defended. The right to assemble publicly, speak freely, bear arms, choose how to worship, and be free from unreasonable search and seizure by the government is what has made this a country of successful entrepreneurs, of great churches, of amazing charitable institutions, and of proactive civic organizations of all kinds. It is the reason everyone wants to come here.

Ephesians 5:1 says that it is for freedom that God has set us free. It is because we are a nation founded on biblical principles that we *have* our Bill Of Rights and the freedoms it guarantees. But let me play at being C. S. Lewis for a minute and put some new words in old Screwtape's mouth. (If you have never read Lewis' classic work, *The Screwtape Letters,*[4] you should. The premise is that one of Satan's upper level demons is writing letters to a rookie demon, instructing him in the tricks of the trade; how to cleverly lead his "client" [you] away from God.) Here's Uncle Screwtape's latest missive to his bumbling nephew, as intercepted and translated by me.

> Foolish Wormwood! You are discouraged because your client has discovered that his religion is not about rules and regulations, but that he has been set free! Were you asleep during your history classes? Have you forgotten our incredible success in the matter of the Bill of Rights? How we cleverly perverted the obnoxiously freeing language of that document by inserting into the

minds of millions of Americans the idea that defending their rights was a higher good than fulfilling their responsibilities? Notice especially how we subtly expanded in their imaginations the rights they were actually given in the Constitution until they thought they had the right to be fed without working, to be respected without earning respect, to be heard when they had nothing to say, to be praised even when they were wrong, and to know things that were none of their business. "Inquiring minds want to know" was one of Scrimpshard's most glorious triumphs.

Use these principles on your client. Blur in his mind what it is he has been set free from. Confusion about sin is always to be desired. Hold before him constantly the alluring pictures of "freedom" in the worldly sense—no limits, no responsibilities—so that he may lose sight of the distressing fact that he has been set free to serve, to sacrifice, and to seek the face of our great Enemy.

The devil has done his work well in America. We think we have the right to be happy. Even the Constitution only mentions the right to *pursue* that illusive goal.

If we find ourselves in a marriage that is not completely fulfilling and "happy," we think we have the "right" to walk away from it, regardless of the cost to others. Our right to be happy trumps our responsibility to fulfill a vow made not just to another person but to God.

Our "right" to have all the things we want trumps our responsibility to be good stewards and live within the means God has provided.

Our "right" to say exactly what we think in every situation trumps our responsibility to put the needs and feelings of others above our own.

Have you ever thought about which of your rights are truly inalienable (can never be taken from you)? Imagine yourself born in China or as a woman in Afghanistan. What if you were a missionary kidnapped by mercenary rebels in the Philippines? What if you were an unborn child in America? The right to life, liberty, and the pursuit of happiness would be out the window in all those situations. Free speech would certainly not in the picture. All the rest of our cherished American rights would have been vaporized, too.

What you are left with, then, is the right to die and the right to worship God in your heart. Those two things can never be taken away from you.

Remember that each of those rights granted us in the Constitution comes balanced by a responsibility. Do we want to retain the right to vote? We'd better use it. Do journalists want to retain freedom of the press? They'd better not abuse it by printing any national security secrets they unearth. Do we want to retain the right to public assembly? Best avoid rioting in the streets. These and many others are just our civic responsibilities. Our responsibilities as Christians to be salt and light in a dark world are even more important. Salt preserves, light shows the way, and the world *will* be watching.

Feeding Stinky Sheep

I have said that forgiveness and gentle speech are two of the areas where people perceive disunity between Christian belief and action. Another is the matter of servanthood. Remember when Jesus washed the disciples' feet? He said He came not to be served but to serve, and we are supposed to be striving to be more and more Christlike. I guess He was leading by example.

Some of His last instructions to His disciples were about this matter of servanthood. He told them to feed His sheep. It wasn't a third or fourth hand directive. He didn't say, "I want you to be generous in giving to programs that study the problem of the nutritional requirements of sheep." He said to Peter, "Feed my sheep." And He said it three times to make sure Peter who, like us, was sometimes a bit dense got the message.

That passage is full of many-layered meanings. It echoes the three times Peter denied Him, for instance. The Bible is multi-dimensional, which is why we need to continue to read it regularly. No one could possibly understand it all after just one reading.

So who are the sheep? Well, I'm one of the dumb, stubborn, bleating little idiots, and so are you. We are to serve one another and be good Samaritans to the whole world.

Is that what the world sees when it looks at us? Sometimes. If they know their history, they will have noticed that the US, a nation based on biblical principles, is unique in the world, in that when we fight another country, destroying their infrastructure, instead of imposing tribute, we come in and try to help them rebuild.

Some of the most effective humanitarian aid programs in the world are run by Christians as para-church organizations. Franklin Graham's Samaritan's Purse does untold good around the world in a number of different ways, as do various child support organizations. But again, just as with forgiveness, what does the secular world really look at? They are watching the up-close and personal. They are watching how we serve each other. Here is a very partial list of people that both you and the secular world can look to as models of Christian service.

- Mother Teresa, who personally did whatever it took to save the street children of Calcutta.
- The hundreds of volunteers who, with no fanfare or attention, take wonderful care of young women in the Gabriel Project.
- The woman (there's at least one in every church) who is always the last to leave after any function, because she has made sure the kitchen was left clean.
- Our friends and neighbors who have taken aging or dying relatives into their homes to care for. My personal hero in that category is Cecelia Garcia.
- People like my friend, Marilyn Anderes, who does whatever it takes to show the women she is mentoring how much she and God care for them, including scrubbing their toilets, if that is what's needed.

So sometimes, if they are looking at the right people, the world *does* see Christians modeling love and service. Think what a huge impact it might have if every single Christian would lay down the idea that she had a right to be served and focused on what her friends, brothers and sisters in Christ, neighbors, and community needed and then acted to meet that need.

Heroes Are Important

During World War II, the Germans were using a bombing blitzkrieg to soften Britain up for an invasion. There is still a half-wrecked church right next to the parliament building in London. The destruction was general. From tenements to mansions and ancient castles, there were no safe places anywhere in Britain, but London was the most dangerous place to be. The children were evacuated en masse into the country. The king and queen stayed. One bomb missed the king and queen by only a few hundred feet. Their example of bravery and dogged determination was a great inspiration to the British people and to the world.

Let me tell you a little about George Washington, the father of our country, who is much under-rated in current history books. I'll be quoting from Peter Marshall's great book, *The Light and the Glory*, and from General Washingtons's own writings. This is from Washington's own handwritten prayer diary.

> Let my heart, therefore, gracious God, be so affected with the glory and majesty of thine honor that I may not do mine works, but wait on

thee, and discharge those weighty duties which
thou requirest of me.

Another day he wrote:

Direct my thoughts, words and work, wash away
my sins in the immaculate Blood of the Lamb,
and purge my heart by the Holy Spirit...daily
frame me more and more into the likeness of thy
son, Jesus Christ.[5]

I thought these words were important because it
is currently popular among historians—who are the
people who write your children's history books—to
portray Washington not as a Christian but a deist.
That is, believing there is a God but not in Jesus as a
personal savior or in the concept of the Trinity. They
conclude this from the fact that in public speeches
he often referred to "the Divine" or to "Providence"
rather than to Christ. I think these prayers, recorded
in his own hand, disprove that theory pretty effectively. Now listen to how this brave Christian man
led his troops and his country by example.

Speaking of the terrible winter at Valley Forge,
The Light and the Glory says:

But Washington did not spare himself. Early in
the morning, he would begin making the rounds
of the camp, and would spend most of the day

riding from one regiment to the next, talking to the men. As Dr. Thatcher commented: "The army...was not without consolation, for his excellency, the commander in chief...manifested a fatherly concern and fellow feeling for their sufferings and made every exertion in his power to remedy the evil and administer the much desired relief."[6]

Conditions at the encampment of the army at Valley Forge grew worse and worse, but it forged a core of men committed to the cause of liberty and to the general who led them. Quoting again from, *The Light and the Glory*:

This then was the miracle of Valley Forge. That the men endured was indeed amazing to all who knew the circumstances. But the reason they endured—the reason they believed in God's deliverance was simple. They could believe, because their general did believe.

Where historians credit Washington for things, Washington himself credited God. In telling his troops that the French had come down as our allies and were sending help, he said

It having pleased the Almightly Ruler of the universe to defend the cause of the United

American States, and finally to raise up a powerful friend among the princes of the earth...it becomes us to set apart a day for gratefully acknowledging the divine goodness and celebrating the important event which we owe to His divine interposition. [5]

It was not in prayer and fine words alone that Washington led. Listen to this firsthand account of a time later in the war.

They caught up with the British at Monmouth, and Charles Lee...permitted Wayne to engage the enemy, but as soon as the British turned to fight, Lee ordered a general retreat.

Furious, Washington spurred to the front of his own column, summarily relieved Lee of command, and rescued his forces from impending disaster. Back and forth he rode on his big gray, calmly urging the men to re-form, and giving them the example of his own quiet courage in the midst of withering fire. No man could look at him that day and not take heart. The troops stopped, turned and fought the British to a standstill, causing them to grudgingly fall back. From that time the British never made the mistake of underestimating their opponents.[6]

Make sure your children don't learn everything they know about the father of our country from the public school history books. This man is a worthy role model for the young people of our country. Until September 11 of 2001, it was popular in our culture to tear down heroes, to find flaws in them and insinuate that the flaws invalidated the greatness. This is where a Christian worldview stands us in good stead. We know that all have sinned and fallen short of the glory of God. The fact that our heroes are flawed makes it all the more praiseworthy that they have heard and heeded the call to come higher, achieve more, trust God.

Role models of Washington's stature are not a dime a dozen. The world was watching him. The world was watching the king and queen of England during World War II. The world was watching Mordecai. At least parts of the world are watching you.

Laying A Foundation

It is incumbent on us to lead by example, but we are not alone. We can use the lives of all who have gone before, holding them up to be studied. Remember, that in Acts 7, Timothy, called before the council to defend his faith, used not only what he himself had seen and witnessed but the whole history of the Jewish people.

In Hebrews 11, Paul went through a whole roll call of people God had used as examples of what he was talking about. He ended up with that wonderful phrase in Hebrews 12:1, "Since we are surrounded by so great a cloud of witnesses, let us also lay aside every weight, and sin which clings so closely, and let us run with perseverance the race that is set before us".

One of the last things Moses did before taking a long look at the Promised Land (which he would never set foot in) and surrendering his soul to God was to repeat for the whole tribe, one last time, the history of their nation. (See the Book of Deuteronomy.)

When Paul was called upon to speak in the synagogue at Antioch, he prefaced the gospel by laying down a foundation of history.

I think it is important to lay a foundation of knowledge about great men and women of faith for our children. That means first acquiring it for ourselves. When we start learning about these people, we will find our own faith strengthened, our witness clarified, and our courage augmented. We will start to be able to see the army of invisible hosts, which makes it true to say that those who are with us are more than those who are with the world. Peterson translates the phrase, "Lord God of hosts," as "God of the angel armies." I really like that. When you see how great men and women have risen above what would seem to be possible in their mortal strength, you will see that they were strengthened by the God of the angel armies.

Remember what the historian said about the troops at Valley Forge, that they were *able* to believe in God's deliverance because their general *did* believe. Those who look to you will be able to believe if they see that you believe. Pray for God to bless you with wisdom. James says to. Pray to be blessed with courage and conviction. Pray that you will be strengthened to set a good example. There is nothing wrong with praying for the Lord to bless you. It's not selfish. It's just practical. How can He use you to bless others if He hasn't first blessed you?

If you are to be one of the Christlike examples that the world can look at and see integrity—organic unity of faith and action—, you must grow in your knowledge of the Word and in your submission to God's will. You must give away some rights.

As Galatians 5:13 says, "For you were called to freedom, brethren; only do not use your freedom as an opportunity for the flesh, but through love be servants of one another."

DISCUSSION QUESTIONS

1. Who has been a shining example to you in your life?

   _____

   _____

   _____

   _____

   _____

2. What historical or famous figures have inspired you?

   _____

   _____

   _____

   _____

   _____

3. Have you ever found out later that something you did or said made a difference in someone's life?

   _____

   _____

   _____

   _____

   _____

4. What do you think is the biggest impediment to your having a "servant's heart?"

_____

_____

_____

_____

_____

_____

5. Can you identify any areas where you have mis-judged what your rights are?

_____

_____

_____

_____

_____

_____

6. Read Matthew 6:12–15. What importance did Jesus place on forgiveness? Who do you need to forgive? (Clue: there is probably more than one.)

_____

_____

_____

_____

_____

_____

CHAPTER 5

COUNT THE COST, THEN ACT

When Haman's plot became public, Mordecai laid the impending disaster before Esther, told her she was her people's only hope, and that perhaps she was put there for such a time as this.

For Esther, the possible cost of what she was about to do was clear. If the king wasn't in a great mood when she tiptoed unbidden into his august presence, it could have been "off with her head!" So she didn't charge in blindly. She stopped to count the cost.

This is an excellent precedent for us. It can work in two directions. It may so firm our faith in what we are about to do that we straighten our backs, lift our chins, and say with Esther, "If I die, I die."

Or, it may give that moment's reflection during which God's Holy Spirit whispers, "Better not." It can give time to realize that we are stubbornly set to do something totally wrong or foolish. It can give us time to check our motivation—the subject of the next lesson. All of God's precepts—the guidelines He gives us for living a good life fit so immaculately together that it is difficult to separate one teaching from another. If you notice, as you read this chapter, you will see a striking resemblance to the table of contents for the whole book.

It's All Connected

If you want to know something about an artist, you start by studying his art. Similarly, much can be learned about how God fits everything together by studying His creation. At first glance you see a lot of separate things. There's a tree. There's a bird. There's a bee. There's a flower. You can learn a lot from studying these things. Each one is a miracle of complexity. But as you move back from a detailed study of individuals, you start to get a bigger picture, and you realize that it is all hooked together irreducibly.

Just the obvious surface interdependency of creation, the part that you learn in grade school, is amazing. I've learned to watch for reflections of the things God did in creating the universe in the ways

He works in our lives. I was therefore not surprised to find many of the ways to count the cost of a proposed action reflected in the other lesson topics. All God's lessons are complex and inter-related.

Why?

Before tackling *how* to count the cost, I want to cover *why* to do it. We've talked about the first why: Quiet consideration allows time to stiffen your courage for the task ahead, or alternately, to realize you are about to take the wrong road—a dead end, one full of potholes, or one leading away from God. Another reason is that God didn't give us brains just to keep our skulls from collapsing. We're supposed to use them.

Listen to what C. S. Lewis says in *Mere Christianity*. He is talking about the four Cardinal Virtues, one of which is Prudence.

> Prudence means practical common sense, taking the trouble to think out what you are doing and what is likely to come of it. Nowadays most people hardly think of Prudence as one of the virtues. In fact, because Christ said we could only get into His world by being like children, many Christians have the idea that as long as you are "good," it does not matter being a fool. But that is a misunderstanding.

In the first place children show plenty of prudence about doing the things they are really interested in, and think them out quite sensibly. In the second place, as St. Paul points out, Christ never meant that we were to remain children in intelligence: on the contrary, He told us to be not only "harmless as doves" but also "as wise as serpents." He wants a child's heart but a grown-up's head. He wants us to be simple, single minded, affectionate and teachable, as good children are; but He also wants every bit of intelligence we have to be alert at its job, and in first class fighting trim. The fact that you are giving money to a charity does not mean that you need not find out whether that charity is a fraud or not.

He has room for people with very little sense, but he wants everyone to use what sense they have…. God is no fonder of intellectual slackers than of any other slackers. If you are thinking of becoming a Christian, I warn you that you are embarking on something that is going to take the whole of you, brains and all.[1]

God expects us to use all the gifts He's given us, and our brains are one of them. So, the second reason to count the cost, is because God expects you to. In Luke 14:28–30, Jesus said, "For which of you, desiring to build a tower, does not first sit down and count the cost. Whether he has enough to complete it? Otherwise, when he has laid the foundation, and is not able to finish, all who see mock him, saying, 'this man began to build and was not able to finish.'"

At first blush, this (so we won't appear foolish) does not seem to be a godly reason for counting the cost. One of the reasons God loved King David was that he didn't mind appearing foolish before men as he danced wholeheartedly at the front of the procession that brought the Ark of the Covenant into Jerusalem.

Here we are at balance again. Is the thing foolish, or does it just *appear* so to men? Whatever men may say, it is not foolish to praise God and to rejoice at joyful events. It is *not* foolish to act uprightly in accordance with your Scripture-sharpened conscience, as we talked about in chapter two, even when that seems to be to your immediate disadvantage. It *is* foolish to jump into water over your head when you know you can't swim—and that is what it is like to start something you know you don't have the resources to finish.

If we consistently do things that are truly foolish, we are not being a good example. The world will look at us to get an idea of what it means to be a Christian and all it will see is foolishness. Instead of saying, "This wise and prudent person thinks it's a good idea to praise and serve God," they will think, "This God-stuff is just more of her foolishness."

Reviewing, we stop to count the cost in order 1) to brace ourselves and rally our courage, 2) to give ourselves time to hear the Holy Spirit speaking to us in His still small voice, 3) in obedience because God has told us to be wise and use our brains, and 4) in order that the world may observe that Christians are wise, not foolish.

How?

I cannot tell you how many times I have been saved from falling into big trouble by one little thought: "I'd better check this with Johny." We are not admonished to submit to our husbands in order to make them our rulers but in order for them to fulfill their God-given responsibility of protecting us.

We all know that men's minds work differently from ours. This is no longer an anecdotal old wives tale but documented fact. You can see it on electroencephalograms. That can be very frustrating when we think we're having a meaningful conversation only to find out later that neither of us had any idea what the other one was talking about. It can also be our salvation when our husband, father, or pastor sees a pitfall to which we were totally oblivious.

The first way of counting the cost is to check in with your husband, if you have one. If the Lord hasn't see fit to provide one, or if he's gone on home ahead of you, and the matter under advisement is something such as which new coat to buy, you can probably wing it. But if it has life-changing implications, you might want to get that male perspective from someone in your family or church whose intelligence and honesty you respect, just to make sure you're not at the edge of one of those pitfalls visible only to a man. Offer to reciprocate. *We* can see ones they are likely to miss.

One of my reader/advisors said a wise thing. She said that when making decisions about her children she always asks herself, "What will be the consequences in twenty years?" Of course, you can't always know. The future is not given to us to see. But common sense, experience, and observation can often give you a clue. Therein lies the second step: think out the probable consequences.

Remember when David finally realized that he had sinned grievously against God in the matter of Uriah and Bathsheba? Part of his prayer, after he had prostrated himself before God and felt assured of forgiveness, was " if I had cherished iniquity in my heart, God would not have listened" (Psalm 66:18). He was thinking out consequences. Lack of repentance leads to God not listening to you. Too bad he didn't stop to count the cost *before* he did it, thereby eliminating the necessity to repent. It is never to late, this side of the grave, to fall on God's mercy, trust in the grace of Jesus' salvation, and be forgiven. It is, however, often too late to avert the consequences. This whole lesson is about getting you to think through the possible consequences *before* you act.

My Friend Susie

Here is Susie's calendar for next week.

Tuesday	Wednesday	Thursday	Friday
cookies for field Trip	meg to Alice's -7:30	clean for Friday	MOPS 9:30 -11:30
playdate/lunch w/Amanda	jimmy's field trip 8-5		cook
soccer 3:30	pick up Meg	Meg's Ballet 3:30-4:30	6:00 Brownie & Young's to dinner
small group at Chris' 7:30		PTA meeting 7:00	

It is Tuesday. Susie and her husband have set a priority of always sitting down as a family for dinner, so while it's not on the calendar, remember that Susie has to make a decision each day about what to serve and do some kind of preparation. On Wednesday she could throw a one-pot meal in the crock-pot before leaving to accompany her son on the field trip, or she could stop for pizza on the way home, but she must do something. Eating dinner and cleaning up will take at least an hour.

You've got the picture of her week in your mind. Let's say her best friend calls early Tuesday and says, "Let's ride over to the outlets on the Eastern Shore on Thursday morning. We can get an early start on Christmas." What would be the probable consequences if she says, "Great," and jumps in her car? Right. When is she going to clean and make the dessert for that house full of people she is expecting Friday night? Think out the probable consequences.

As Esther was thinking out the probable consequences, there were two equally likely scenarios. The king, who was fond of her, might hold out his scepter, invite her into the throne room, and she could proceed with her plan. Or the king, who was a proud man and fond of his own reputation, might decide she was as pushy and uppity as Vashti and banish or even execute her.

She decided the risk was worth it. Maybe Susie will decide that the risk of not being able to snatch enough fifteen-minute segments in which to get the house presentable is worth it for the pleasure of her friend's company and the advantage of getting a jump on the Christmas shopping. Especially if her friend has been going through some rough times and really needs a day out. The trick here is to make an informed decision. Think about it. *Know* the probable consequences so you can decide whether it's worth it.

A third thing to consider when counting the cost is whether it will compromise the integrity of your witness. Say you have a neighbor whom you have taken to your church a few times. You are working up your courage to talk to her about your faith and the impact it has had on your life. What would the probable consequences be if you repeated to a third party some juicy detail of her life told to you in confidence? Such things have a way of getting back to people. Would she be much impressed with anything you subsequently told her about Jesus?

You can see how "probable consequences" is going to appear in almost all the ways of counting the cost.

What if your old college buddy was getting married and into the girls' night-out party thrown in her honor there strutted a good-looking, well-defined hunk of a guy who turned on his boom box and started to dance and strip?

Do you murmur in the bride's ear, "I love you, I'll see you Saturday, but I'm outta here"? If you don't do that, and if it gets back to the people who look to you to see what a Christian looks like that you were cheering and laughing with the rest of them, will your witness have the same impact it had before? Probably not.

There may also be a loyalty/faithfulness issue to consider. If Susie's husband is very laid back about the house, then it's pretty much up to Susie whether or not to take that risk. But if she knows that it would distress him to have their friends visit a less-than-perfectly clean house that pops another factor into her decision making. She has to be considerably more sure she'll be able to work the cleaning in.

The loyalty factor doesn't just apply in marriage. If someone at work wants you to do something underhanded—not record all the tips taken in at waitressing, cheat on the cash register, or cover for them when they sneak things out of inventory you have three loyalty questions to deal with. Foremost is loyalty to God. He has delineated His position pretty clearly on not stealing, cheating, or using false scales (see the whole book of Proverbs). The second factor is loyalty to your government. Some of those things are tax evasion. Finally, you must consider loyalty to your employer, who is the one being cheated.

Another major element of counting the cost involves attention to detail: reading the fine print. You must literally *read the fine print* in your insurance contracts, the waiver the doctor or surgeon asks you to sign, the warrantee for whatever you're buying, or the contract you sign to get work done on your house or your car.

True Confessions

As I mentioned before, I am not the poster child for attention to detail. Had I remained unmarried or been stupid enough to marry anyone else, I'm sure I would have been cheated and scammed out of thousands of dollars by now. Additionally, I would have failed to collect thousands that were due me. But the Lord provided mightily for me when he sent a young GAO investigative auditor across the state of Missouri to stay at the motel where I was lifeguarding for the summer. (That's the best I've ever looked in my whole life. Poor man; it's the only time in his life he ever fell for false advertising.) And now God has sent me to tell you what I've learned from Johny about being wise as serpents when dealing with the world.

A friend of ours was considering buying a home safe in which to keep records, some valuable jewelry, a little extra cash, etc. He was impressed when the salesman told him that there was a fifty thousand-dollar insurance policy that came with the safe. All you had to do was send in an inventory each year to keep their records updated, and in case anything was destroyed by fire, you would be compensated up to fifty thousand dollars.

When Johny read the fine print for him, it turned out to cover only two hundred and fifty dollars worth of bonds and cash. There was a five hundred-dollar limit on each piece of jewelry, and a one thousand-dollar total limit on jewelry. Additionally, you needed an appraisal for each piece of jewelry, and of course, you'd better have *that* stored somewhere besides the safe or anywhere else in your burned-down house. So what exactly does this policy cover? What in the world else might you have in that safe that would need insuring? Fifty thousand dollars worth of free insurance sure sounds good, but you really only got $1,250 dollars worth, and a thousand of that required outside documentation.

Well, the whole point of having a safe is to guard against robbery and fire. They are heat resistant, and likely your things would not be destroyed; and if they were, your homeowner's insurance would probably cover it, but you'd better read the fine print there, too. This is a perfect story to illustrate the point that even honest salesmen often don't know what they're talking about, and if you don't want to be foolish, you need to check the details for yourself. Proverbs 14:15 says, "The simple believes everything, but the prudent looks where he is going."

What about the contract to have an addition put on your house? Is the contractor responsible for moving the shrubs that will be in the way, or are you? Is the builder liable if he damages part of the existing structure, or is there a cleverly worded waiver in there somewhere?

Delays are a universal complaint in this sort of situation. If there is a delay due to weather, that's understandable. But if you don't see those guys again until three weeks after the rain quits, you can bet that's because they are catching up at the house where the homeowner inserted a deadline date, after which the contractor would pay a daily or weekly penalty for non-completion. *No problemo* (to him) if yours is a little late.

Aaack!

I can hear the wheels grinding out there. You are thinking, "How can I possibly know all this stuff?" That question brings us to another lesson taught in Esther: check with the folks who know the territory.

Try to imagine the king's harem. The instruction was to gather all the beautiful young women in all the provinces of Persia. I don't even want to guess how many that was, but I think "lots" would be a safe description.

They didn't really have any demands put on them for a whole year. It was kind of like a free year at one of those Ritzy California beauty spas—they were massaged, mud- and myrrh-bathed, coifed and perfumed, and pampered within an inch of their sanity. I don't know about you, but at fourteen through eighteen, which is about the age these girls were, I could have gotten into that—for about a week. Then I would have wanted to be doing something. But they couldn't!

Do you think there might have been some rivalries develop? Some snits, some treacheries? Were you ever seventeen?

Finally the big night came. They could take anything and as much of it as they wanted with them when they went to see the king. Can't you see them all trying to outdo each other?

"I'm going to take a zither player and some incense."

"Well, I'm going to have a string quartet, one of those perfumed oil lamps, and a big plate of divinity."

"I'm going to sing for him and have a five-piece eunuch-boy band to back me up, and I'm going to wear pale pink silk veils with jewels sewed on them."

What did Esther do? She asked the chief eunuch, "What should I take?", and that's all she took. How wise she was. There's a pretty good chance that this guy knew what the king liked.

So how do you count the cost by paying attention to detail when you don't even know where to start? You check with the people who know the territory. Before you sign a contract with a builder, talk to everybody you know who has put an addition on their house. Find out what can go wrong.

Before you base your decision to buy one car instead of another on a superior warrantee, read the fine print in the warrantee and talk to some people who own one to see how the company backs up their promises. Go to the library and check out the research in *Consumer's Digest*.

Doing this kind of homework is a part of attention to detail, which is part of counting the cost, 'cause God said to use your brains so you wouldn't appear foolish, so your witness wouldn't be compromised, so ...did I mention it was all very interconnected?

Because ...

Another part of counting the cost is checking your motivation. There are many verses that apply here. One is, "man looks on the outward appearance, but the lord looks on the heart" (I Samuel 16: 7b). So, it's your motivation that is important to God.

If Susie chooses not to go shopping on Tuesday out of respect for her husband's feelings and a sincere desire to serve and be a blessing to the people she has invited into her home, that's a good decision. If she ignores her friend's very real need for some quality time because she wants to show off a "perfect" house to people she only invited over to impress the socks off, that's a bad decision. Your motivation makes all the difference.

First Corinthians 13 says that if you do all kinds of good things but lack love, (read proper motivation) then you're just a clanging gong, a nothing, because God looks on the heart. We'll cover *how* to check your motivation and some common misconceptions in the next lesson.

Show Me the Money

The question "What is the cost?" must also be addressed very literally. Can you afford to do it? Do you have the resources? If Susie and her husband have just $100 dollars a month beyond regular expenses and are putting half of that away for emergencies and the other half into a college fund for their children, tempting herself by going to the outlets doesn't seem very smart. If getting together with her friend passes all the other tests but fails this one, maybe she could suggest coffee in the kitchen over some Christmas idea magazines so they can plan some inexpensive gifts they could *make*.

Also remember that if you owe money, your "extra" is not your own until you have repaid your debt. It doesn't matter if it's five dollars you owe your sister, five hundred dollars you owe your parents, or five thousand dollars you have accrued in credit card debt. Proverbs 12:9 says, *"Better is a man of humble standing who works for himself than one who plays the great man but lacks bread"* (Italics mine). If you owe large credit card debt, you are not working for yourself. You may be "playing the big man" with all the stuff you have acquired, but you are working just to pay the interest. The cost of every item you charge goes up twelve to eighteen percent monthly if you cannot pay off the entire balance every billing period. If you charge a super fifty-percent-off deal but go three months without paying for it, your discount is gone, and you are paying more than full retail price.

I know I sound like Larry Burkett, and if these kinds of concepts are something you struggle with, I recommend his books. The principles they teach are sound both financially and biblically.

The Big Picture

Finally, when counting the cost, you need to ask whether whatever you are about to embark on will glorify God. Is this the best use of your resources? Your money, sure, but more importantly, your time and your energy. It helps here if you have some idea of where God is sending you.

In *My Utmost for His Highest*[2] Oswald Chambers says, "Every person is grasped by Christ for some purpose; and therefore every person should all his life press on so that he may grasp that purpose for which Christ grasped him".

In discussing this concept with my small group, we decided it's really hard to know exactly what God's purpose is for our lives. Even when we think we know, we are probably only seeing the next mile on the journey. The important thing is to keep focused on the fact that He does have a purpose, a very personal, specific purpose for *your* life.

When Joseph was down in that well, he didn't have a clue where God was taking him. When he was a slave in Potipher's house, the big picture was not something he could see. And when he was in prison, it must have been even dimmer. It wasn't until his brothers showed up looking for famine relief that it became clear to him, and he was able to say, "you meant evil against me, but God meant it for good." (Genesis 49:20).

But, during the years when he couldn't see the big picture, Joseph was faithful to what he *did* know. God says, work hard, do your best (everything as unto the Lord), and Joseph did that. God says lying with somebody else's wife is a no-no, so Joseph ran for his life when Potipher's wife tried to seduce him. Remember the part about how doing what is right may not always be to our immediate advantage? It got Joseph thrown into jail, where he still worked hard. In the end he was mightily used by God.

So, …you're muddling along, trying to count the cost of something, and you remember to ask, "Does it glorify God? Does it fit in with God's plan for my life?" But you don't *know* God's plan for your life, because He works like the CIA, on a need-to-know basis.

In her wonderful book, *The Hiding Place*[3], Corrie ten Boom described a time when she was going on a train trip and her father didn't give her the tickets until she was stepping on to the train. Her point was that God will provide what you need when you need it—usually not before. Say to yourself, "I don't know all of God's plan for my life. What *do* I know?"

I have said many times (and nobody has ever risen up and said, "Oh no, not me!") that every Christian knows, if she is honest, that there is something that God is calling her to do that she has not yet done. I guess it's possible to be in that delicious state where you have finally scrambled up onto a step you've been struggling with but God has not yet fully illuminated the next one. Even then, you usually know there *is* a next one.

Maybe He's calling you to be more of a servant or to quit smoking. Perhaps you feel the call to be studying His Word more faithfully or to become more physically fit, 'cause there's a task ahead that will require it. Is there a broken relationship He's telling you to mend? Does He want you to control your smart mouth? The list is as varied as God's people are.

The point is to ask yourself, "Is this thing that I am contemplating going to get in the way? Is it another stumbling block or excuse not to work on the thing I know God is calling me to?"

Remember that bit in the second chapter about Scotty not being able to beam you up the mountain? If you don't deal with the thing God's calling you to do, you'll never get any closer to the top. If Corrie hadn't packed her bags, combed her hair, and gone to the station but just sat in the living room, demanding to see the tickets, she never would have taken the trip.

Be strong and DO it

The final step in the process is to act. As my friend, Val Archer, put it, "If you count the cost long enough, you can avoid doing anything at all." Remember the story of my grandmother and the ice cream? There comes a point where you add up all your cost counting and follow David's advice to Solomon, *"Be strong and do it."* That can be a matter of days or in the case of some really big decisions, months. Or it can be a few seconds, but between the counting and the acting should always be the indispensable step of praying. Ask God for His input and commit your efforts to Him. God will not despise any sincere prayer for guidance offered up to Him in His Son's name. It can be as simple and childlike as, "Hold my hand. Here I go."

It does behoove us, however, to apply all our understanding to a thing as important as prayer and to strive to grow and mature in this vital component of our spiritual lives. There are a lot of wonderful books about prayer, and I have listed some of my favorites in the bibliography. There are many wonderful prayers recorded in the Bible, including the Lord's Prayer in Matthew 5 and Jesus' high priestly prayer, recorded in John 17, where He prayed for *us* you and me—as well as for the apostles who surrounded Him.

The thrust of John Bunyon's little book, *How to Pray in the Spirit*, is that you can pray in your own words and that God wants to hear it all. This flew in the face of the Church's accepted wisdom at that time. They taught people to memorize and recite prayers provided to them by the Church. If you have read that quote from Bunyon a few times as I suggested, you have probably noticed that he wrote the book from Bedford Prison, where he also penned *The Pilgrim's Progress*. He was there because he wouldn't stop preaching that people could approach God without the help of the Church.

There is a well-known acronym for remembering some important elements of prayer. It is ACTS: Adoration, Confession, Thanksgiving, and Supplication, which basically means bringing your concerns. It's a good guide, but don't let anybody's guidelines or your own feelings of inadequacy keep you from praying when you need to pray. If your child is drowning, you probably only have time to think, "Help me, Lord" as you jump into the water, but you sure don't want to fail to ask for help.

The call to pray about decisions doesn't just apply to what the world would consider "important" ones. Let me put some words in Susie's mouth. Her prayer before calling her friend with a yes or no might sound some thing like this: "Dear Father, glorious Creator of all that is, I am coming to You in Your Son's name—the only way I dare to come. You know I have messed up a lot. I really want to walk more in Your ways, and I have used the brains You gave me to think this through, and I think I know what You would have me do. If I've missed something here, please bring it to mind. If I've misjudged my motives, I ask you to search me and to give me a clean heart. I thank You, Father, for the luxury of having such decisions to make. Thank You for my husband, my family, and my friends. I've given my life to You, Lord Jesus, and I ask again that You would use me to bless these people. In Jesus' name, Amen."

Whatever her decision, after counting the cost and praying, she then has to "be strong and do it."

DISCUSSION QUESTIONS

1. Are you a person who counts the cost, or do you tend to leap before you look?

   _____

   _____

   _____

   _____

   _____

2. Have you ever known someone who went through a hard time that could have been avoided by taking time to think through the consequences?

   _____

   _____

   _____

   _____

   _____

3. Can you think of an instance where someone's testimony has been tarnished by his or her foolishness?

   _____

   _____

   _____

   _____

   _____

4. Under what circumstances would you say with Esther, "If I die, I die"?

    _____

    _____

    _____

    _____

    _____

    _____

5. What is the essential step between counting the cost and acting?

    _____

    _____

    _____

    _____

    _____

    _____

6. Have you ever had the problem of counting the cost so long you wound up doing nothing?

    _____

    _____

    _____

    _____

    _____

    _____

CHAPTER 6

CHECKING YOUR MOTIVATION

One of the first verses I found about motivation was Proverbs 21:2, which says, "Every way of a man is right in his own eyes, but God judges the heart." That's pretty clear. It makes you think that checking your motivation might be somewhat important. Verse 27 reads, "The sacrifice of the wicked is an abomination; how much more when he brings it with evil intent."

That muddled me. Why would a person with evil intentions (motivations) be bringing a sacrifice at all? I mulled that over a while but got no closer to clarity until I was walking one morning and started going over in my mind the Sermon on the Mount, which I memorized a few years ago. I try to go over it every couple of weeks so I won't lose it.

Chapter five is the Beatitudes and then all the teachings about Jesus' people not being free from the law, being held not just to the letter but to the spirit of the law, a much higher standard. He gives lots of examples of how He expects more of us. He says, "You've heard…, but I say…," and whatever He says is harder than the original law. For instance, He says, "You have heard that it was said, 'an eye for an eye, and a tooth for a tooth.' But I say to you, do not resist one who is evil. But if anyone strikes you on the right cheek, turn to him the other also" (Mathew 5:38-39). He follows that up by saying to love your enemies and pray for those who spitefully use you. That leads right into chapter six where Jesus says, "Beware of practicing your piety before men in order to be seen by them; for then you will have no reward from your father who is in heaven" (Mathew 6:1). I always want to say "beware of practicing *this* piety," because it clearly refers to what went before.

He elaborates by saying, "Thus when you give alms, sound no trumpet before you, , as the hypocrites do in the synagogues and in the streets, that they may be praised by men. Truly, I say to you, they have received their reward." (Mathew 6:2). He says pretty much the same thing about prayer and about fasting.

Aha! That is how you could be offering a sacrifice with evil intentions: offering it not to make atonement but so that men would praise you. One of the ways God will use your scripture memorization is to give you clarity and balance in figuring out other passages. You can't know at the time you choose to be obedient to God's admonition to write His Word on your heart how He will use that later. It pays to be obedient.

This whole line of thought was sparked by noticing the contrast between Mordecai's and Haman's motives. We are told in Esther 10:3 (the very last verse of the book) what Mordecai's motives were. It says, "For Mordecai the Jew was next in rank to King Aheseurus, and he was great among the Jews and popular with the multitude of his brethren, for he sought the welfare of his people and spoke peace to all his people."

Haman's motives were less praiseworthy. One of them was bigotry. There was bad blood between the Agagites and the Jews. There was also greed and self-aggrandizement. Under the terms of the persecution he had planned, Haman was obligated to pay into the king's treasury ten thousand talents of silver (that's how he talked the king into it); but he himself would have made a lot more than that, because he was to get all the people (who could be sold into slavery) and all their goods.

Chapter five, verses 10–12 indicates he might also have been laboring under a considerable load of pride.

> Nevertheless Haman restrained himself, and went home; and he sent and fetched his friends and his wife, Zeresh. And Haman recounted to them the splendor of his riches, the number of his sons, all the promotions with which the king had honored him, and how he had advanced him above the princes and the servants of the king. And Haman added, "Even Queen Esther let no one come with the king to the banquet she prepared but myself. And tomorrow I am invited by her together with the king."

Let Her Who Boasts....

Bragging is so easy to spot in other people, isn't it? It's harder to pick out in our own stream of words. Where does the line between bragging and legitimate celebration of a good thing lie?

Being a sports fan, I came up with a football metaphor. Have you ever seen a running back charging down the field, evading the defense, breaking tackles, and bursting triumphantly into the end zone? What he does next draws the line. If he throws the ball into the crowd, goes down on one knee to pray, high-fives his teammates, or throws himself into the stands so that the fans can catch him and cheer, that seems like legitimate celebration. If he turns and struts around, taunting the guy who missed the tackle that would have stopped him, that's bragging, and it isn't pretty.

It's a fine line, because, of course, you want to share good news with family and friends, and you should. Let's take a look at how one event might be handled in several different ways.

Suppose a high school student struggled early in his chemistry class but got help, figured out how to study this difficult subject, and wound up getting an A on his final. Let's say you're his mother. You and your neighbor are taking the trash out at the same time one evening, and she asks, "How's it going?" You say, "Pretty good. I'm really excited, 'cause Billy aced his chem final. Remember I told you he was having a lot of trouble with it last fall? I'm really proud of how hard he worked." Your neighbor smiles and says, "That's great. Tell him I'm really glad for him." You both go back in the house. Sounds like legitimate celebration of a good thing.

Same situation, but this time you are the one who says, "How's it going?"

Your neighbor says, "OK, really, but it looks like Jane will have to go to summer school. She flunked her algebra final and that probably means she will flunk the course."

Do you still share how well Billy did? I don't think so, at least not right then. You might share the name of the tutoring service that was so helpful when he was having trouble but no need to mention the part about his acing the test.

You Ain't Seen Nothing ...

Now let's say Billy is your neighbor's son, and she shares his happy news with you. Is that the best time to mention that your nephew just did really well on his Advanced Placement chemistry test and will be able to go straight into Chemistry 102 next year at *Yale*. Probably not! Let her enjoy the good thing she's celebrating. No need to top it.

Have you noticed our tendency to want to top whatever someone else has said, whether it's a good thing or a bad thing? Sometimes we even say, "You think that's bad? Wait 'til you hear ...", or "I can top that one." It's probably fine if you are telling hilarious stories from the delivery room or regaling each other with tales of travel disasters, but listen to yourself! Make sure you don't squelch other people's joy by topping it.

I was recently talking to a friend who lives in another state, and she was telling me about how impressed she was with her grandson. He was three and a half, was carrying on conversations, and was going from person to person at some large gathering, playing some little imaginary game. I have known three and half year olds who weren't that advanced, so I marveled with her over his brightness and her good fortune to have such a sweet and talented grandbaby. I did *not* mention that my granddaughter, Alli, played tea party with a room full of people, refilling their cups and offering imaginary cake to everyone when she was barely two or that her brother, Bradley, spoke in complete sentences at fourteen months. And it wasn't easy!

Have you spotted any common threads here? There are two. One is immediacy. Once the celebratory spirit fades, you are just bragging. Six-year-old Alli's precociousness at age two is old news. I did share with my friend a cute thing Bradley said recently. There's no competition with her grandbaby there. Bradley is much older.

The other thread is other people's feelings, whether something you say will encourage them or put a damper on their high spirits. Once, when someone was worrying about her child who was having trouble in first grade, I shared the story of Winston Churchill who credited his mastery of the English language to the fact that he had to repeat second grade. No need in a situation like that to talk about the kids in your neighborhood who were reading when they started kindergarten.

Give some thought to whether you take time to share your friends' joys and celebrate with them when good things happen or whether perhaps you need to guard against squelching their joy by topping their story.

Pride Goeth Before ...

Pride was the first un-praiseworthy motive I thought of, because it was so clearly one of Haman's, and bragging is one of the many ways it's displayed. Here's what C. S. Lewis said about pride in *Mere Christianity*.[1]

> According to Christian teachers, the essential vice, the utmost evil, is Pride. Unchastity, anger, greed, drunkenness, and all that are mere fleabites in comparison: it was through pride that the devil became the devil: pride leads to every other vice; it is the complete anti-God state of mind…. A proud man is always looking down on things and people; and of course, as long as you are looking down, you cannot see something that is above you.

So Be It

I was a semi finalist
for the National Merit Scholarship!
I have lots of stuff in my brain.

I know the value of pi
(though I don't recall what to do with it).
I know species and phylums
of plants and animals.
I'm good at finding out
those things I *don't* know.

Is God smiling?
Do we remind Him
of kids playing school?

I don't get why pride
is such an easy sin.
My smarts all amount
to dandelion fluff
in the presence of
His divine intellect.
Blow me away, Lord.

Here's a partial list of some of the kinds of pride
we can fall into.

- Pride of possessions: working so hard to get
  the "stuff" you think you want that you ignore the needs of husband, children, friends,
  or the call of God.
- Pride of place or social status: being a name-
  dropper falls into this category.
- House-proud: when decorating or cleaning

the house starts to seem more important to you than the people in the house.

- Intellectual pride, like the Pharisee in the temple: "O Lord, thank You that I am not stupid like most of these people."
- Pride in your appearance: counting on your looks to get you what you want; being more comfortable relying on your looks than on God.
- Spiritual pride: feeling superior to people who aren't as far along in their walk with the Lord as you are or to people who haven't even realized that they need to be walking with God.

There are probably others. These are just the ones I'm familiar with. I can honestly say I have never been house-proud. I'm familiar with that one through observation, but all the rest I know about because I have wrestled with them myself, like Jacob wrestled with the angel. Here's a tricky thought: what if I became proud of overcoming them? Started looking down on people who haven't overcome them?

If you ask the Lord to keep checking your heart, and if you keep your eyes and ears open for what He might say or show you, you'll become aware of two things that ought to block *that* particular form of pride: 1) the fight isn't over. You'll probably wrestle with it 'til you go home to be with Jesus; 2) Whatever rounds you may have won were not your doing but won in the Lord's strength. The world finds nothing wrong with these forms of pride. In fact, it encourages them, so the Lord *had* to have been strengthening you or you wouldn't even have realized there was an opponent in the ring.

Try to remember 2 Corinthians 10:17, which says, "Let him who boasts, boast of the Lord."

Gimme, Gimme, Gimme!

Another common motive that can lead us astray is greed. We start out as children wanting for ourselves whatever treat the neighbor kids are munching on, and we end up as adults wanting more and more of whatever we want. This often walks hand in hand with pride. People who are house-proud are often greedy to get bigger and bigger houses.

Now there's nothing wrong with having a big house. By American standards, only a few people reading these words will have a really *big* house, but by global standards we all do. An afghan refugee or a poor citizen of New Dehli could get very house-proud over the smallest American apartment. After all, even the oldest, tiniest ones have indoor plumbing, running water, central heating, and electricity. The point is that the term "big" is relative, and it's not how big your house is that makes you a candidate for this kind of pride, it's how you feel about it and how you use it.

While we often see greed hand in hand with pride, it's actually a different thing. It's almost a lust of the mind for whatever the greedy focus has settled on.

Misers are greedy for money. Frugality can be a good thing. Miserliness can't. The frugal person may feed her children potatoes because they're good for them and they're cheap. The miser might divide one potato between three children and give them nothing to put on it because he cannot stand to part with any more of his adored money than is absolutely necessary.

The Devil Is So Dumb!

When I finished that last paragraph, I had what seemed to be an original thought! Many bad things—many sins—are good things taken to extremes or perverted.

I went down my list of bad motives, and sure enough, pride is the perversion of joy in a good thing. Greed is the extreme of frugality. Laziness is a perversion of God's instruction to rest. Revenge and malice are justice taken personally instead of corporately. And despair is the extreme of sorrow, which is a natural and healing emotion when you've suffered loss.

"Wow," I thought, "I am getting really good at this!" Then a little echo of some sort started chiming away in the back of my head. "Deja vu, deja vu." OK, I hear you—where had I read something like that? It came back to me: C. S. Lewis. But try as I might, I couldn't find the reference.

I *did* remember the gist of what he said. It was that the devil couldn't create anything, only God is a creator. Therefore, the devil couldn't make up anything new with which to tempt us away from God. All he could do was twist and pervert and make ugly the good things God has given us.

God made the act of creating a new generation a good and pleasurable thing, and He gave us just one rule: "Only to be used in the context of marriage." The devil worked in our minds to pull it out of its proper context, twist it, mar it, and make it a dirty thing.

The Lord provided the chemical process of fermentation because alcohol is a great disinfectant and a glass of wine now and then is a pleasant thing. Then the devil shoved in and convinced us to use it to such excess that for many people it is necessary to either give it up entirely or live lost and lonely lives at the bottom of a bottle.

The Lord gave us spirits capable of feeling joy and satisfaction. As a small-scale farmer, I know about the satisfaction of working hard and harvesting a good crop. And I know no farmer can do that by himself. If God doesn't send the rain, there will be no harvest.

Luke 12:15–21 says, "And he said to them, 'Take heed, and beware of all covetousness; for a man's life does not consist in the abundance of his possessions.' And he told them a parable, saying, 'The land of a rich man brought forth plentifully; and he thought to himself, "What shall I do, for I have nowhere to store my crops?' And he said, "I will do this: I will pull down my barns, and build larger ones; and there I will store all my grain and goods. And I will say to my soul, Soul, you have ample goods laid up for many years; take your ease, eat, drink, be merry.' But God said to him, 'Fool! This night your soul is required of you; and the things you have prepared, whose will they be?' So is he who lays up treasure for himself, and is not rich toward God."

The devil took the satisfaction, joy, and thankfulness (the farmer didn't do it alone, remember) that were good things and turned them into pride and arrogance. He used them to create a blockade the size of a big old barn between the farmer and God. The man lost sight of the fact that he wasn't immortal, that his life might be required of him at any time.

The Funhouse Mirror

This is the definition of sin: any thought, action, or attitude that separates us from God. Have you ever sat behind someone with a really big hat on or behind a pillar or near a group of rowdy children at some event? That's how the devil works. God is the main event. The devil doesn't want us to even *see* God, let alone get close to Him, so he puts up barriers and sends distractions. Have you heard the saying, "If the devil can't make you bad, he'll make you busy?" Distractions! And all the bad motives—pride, greed, lust, laziness, vengeance, and despair are big old barriers.

They either get in the way of our seeing God, or they distort what we see. There is a lie embedded in each of them that acts like a pane of wavy and distorted glass. What are these lies buried in the bad motives? What truth is the "gold" at the heart of the good ones?

The lie in pride is that we are able to fulfill for ourselves the functions of God in our lives. We are self sufficient and proud of it! The farmer lost sight of the fact that without God's continuing grace he would have grown nothing, no matter how hard he worked at it.

The "gold" in the authentic thing is the ability to take real joy in God's good provisions, knowing they are gifts and none of our doing. Of course we do our part. I have to plant peas in the spring if I hope for God to provide any for the freezer in July, but I can do my part 'til my fingers are worn to the bone, and without God doing His part, it's all for nothing. "Unless the Lord builds the house, those who build it labor in vain," as it says in Psalm 127.

When the satisfaction of having worked hard and well is joined with the knowledge that God blessed your work by doing His part and making it fruitful, that is joy indeed. The psalmist expressed this kind of joy when he said, "This is the day that the Lord has made. I will rejoice and be glad in it."

The lie at the heart of greed is that accumulating the things of this earth will make us secure. Untrue! Tonight our life may be required of us. Or that this material wealth will make us satisfied and happy. Untrue! Proverbs 15:17 says, "Better a meal of herbs where love is, than a fatted ox and hatred with it."

One of the best meals I ever remember eating was a big pot of potato soup. My daddy had been sick and out of work, and the potatoes, one big onion, and can of condensed milk that went into that soup were pretty much all the food we had in the house. But my aunt and my favorite cousin showed up to share it with us. The devil would have you believe that you can only be happy and content in the presence of lots of material possessions. But the Grinch can't steal Christmas, can he? I love it when he's sitting up there on his hill all smug, hoarding the loot he has stolen, but up from the valley trails the sound of Christmas: "Aboo dahmay, welcome Christmas, Christmas day."

What the devil twisted to make greed was frugality, the legitimate pleasure of knowing you have been a good and faithful servant, not wasteful or prodigal with what you've been given. When you do that, you are rewarded, as witnessed in the parable of the talents. Parables are stories meant to apply to broader situations than those portrayed within the confines of the story, but it has to be a true and meaningful story to be a good parable, and Jesus didn't tell any bad parables. So I think it can be taken as meaningful on its face value (it's good to use your resources wisely), as well as for what you can infer from it.

The lie at the heart of lust, which generally involves a physical pleasure, is that if a thing is good, then a lot of it will be even better. If making love is good, then indiscriminate sex will be great. Untrue! It leads only to broken relationships, disease, and children deprived of a stable home.

If food is good, then gluttony will be great. Untrue! It leads to unhealthy bodies and minds that can't focus on God, 'cause they can't quit thinking about food.

Now, I think it's important to say here that just as not everybody who has a large house is house-proud, not everyone who is carrying around some extra pounds has a fixation on food that is keeping them separated from God.

My own struggle with dieting and overweight *were* for many years a big old barrier that I had to fight and claw to look around and see God. I have lost a few pounds since I laid the problem in His lap, and He shattered the big old funhouse mirror I was trying to see Him through, but that was not the point of doing it. If I had done it so that He would let me lose some weight, I would have been mightily disappointed, 'cause it has probably averaged out to about four pounds a year (I can't be sure, because I haven't been on a scale in two years). I don't need to know; that's not what my life is about anymore.

It's also possible to go to the other extreme. Remember that all the bad motivations are good things perverted or taken to extremes. Whether you eat too much or too little, the result is the same: your focus is on your body not on God.

ZZZZZZZZZZZZZ

I don't think I'm far enough out of laziness to see all the lies embedded in it very clearly, but one of them is the assumption that whatever pleasure I am currently enjoying—reading, watching a TV show, sleeping, recreational shopping is more worthy of my time and attention and will lead more surely to a state of personal satisfaction than will stirring my mind to get my body doing whatever work the Lord has called me to.

Maintaining a warm, welcoming, healthy home is an important calling, but my laziness has often made it seem to me like finishing an exciting chapter or getting ten more minutes of sleep would do more for my personal well being than scrubbing the sink or folding the laundry. That's not true! The satisfaction I get from having an orderly home and a well-cared-for family does much more for my self-esteem than finishing that novel ever could.

Rest is "golden," and laziness is a distortion of that. God not only recommends rest, He commands it. One day in seven is for resting. Our bodies need sleep, and our families need some undivided attention. Reading to the kids really is more important the scrubbing the sink. For the mother whose child has been up sick all night, sleeping when the child sleeps isn't lazy, it's smart. She's going to need that renewed energy to take care of the child later. Good grief! We're back to balance again.

"'Vengeance is mine', sayeth the Lord" is probably one of the best known Bible verses, even in the secular world, and boy, we just can't wait to see Him do it! There's an old book where the main character,

Granny Tuttle, says, "Whenever I have a problem, I just hand it over to Providence, and if Providence hasn't done anything about it in 3 or 4 days, I figure He's handed it back to me!"

Justice is the good thing here. But justice, personally administered, is vengeance, and the Lord says that belongs to Him. I think everyone felt compassion for the mother who stood up in open court and shot her child's molester, who seemed to be about to get off lightly. But that was not justice, it was vengeance; and in doing it she finished the wrecking of her family's life that the molester had started.

Doing things out of malice or revenge always wreaks more damage in your own heart, and often in your life, than it inflicts on the people it's aimed at. Justice is good, and we can trust that when it is not administered adequately by our flawed governmental systems, God will pick up the slack. That's the golden truth. The lie is that He needs our help.

I Give Up

The next bad motive I want to address is despair, but a clarification is needed. It is not the same thing as depression. Depression is a complicated thing. It can be the result of lies that the devil planted in your mind during a vulnerable time of trauma, usually in childhood. It can also be the result of a chemical imbalance in your body. In its worst forms, it is often a combination of both of these things.

As women we are better able to empathize with those who suffer from it than men are, because almost all of us have had at least a few experiences of trying to look at the world through smoky, dark "PMS glasses."

When I speak of despair, I am not talking about depression. I know some people who suffer from severe depression who have never allowed despair to overtake them. Even as thoughts that death would be better than what they were experiencing raged through their minds, they clung to the hem of Jesus' garment and continued to believe that God was in control and would ultimately triumph. To paraphrase Dr. V. R. Edman, they never doubted in the dark what God had promised in the light.

I think that is what despair is: giving up on God; the conviction that "this" (whatever it may be) can never be fixed, so there is no point in doing anything. You don't have to be clinically depressed to be a victim of despair. The devil longs to take your sorrow and pain and twist it into despair. Pray! Pray! Pray! Read the Psalms! Sing! Don't let him lie to you. Ask the Lord to restore your joy, which, paradoxically, is not the same as taking away your sorrow.

Grief and sorrow are part of life. Jesus grieved over the death of Lazarus. He grieved over the necessity of the cross. He asked God if there wasn't another way. God will use grief and sorrow to dig deeper places in our souls to pour His love into. He will use them to help us grow wiser as long as we don't fall into despair by believing the lie that "all is lost." Hope is what we have in Jesus. Peter tells us to always be prepared to give a defense for the hope that is within us. Jesus *is* that hope and is the opposite of despair. We can conquer despair by clinging to the hope of Jesus.

That's just an overview of the difference between right and wrong motives. It's no doubt flawed and incomplete, because it is taken only from what I know.

Method One: Pray

There are some effective methods for checking your own motivation, and there are also some popular misconceptions. My number one piece of advice for checking your motives turns out to be my number one piece of advice for almost everything. Pray!

There are only a few exceptions. If you go out the front door one morning and there is a skunk in your yard, my number one piece of advice is close the door, *then* pray.

The very best way to check your motives is to ask God to search your heart and show you what

He finds. This quote from John Calvin gives some practical advice about prayer. He was born in 1509 and only lived to be fifty-five years old, but his writings have had massive influence. Some people think he was a tad on the legalistic side of the perfect balance between law and love, and I can't really say I disagree with them, but this particular writing of his is just great.

> The proper thing is for us always to think of God, and pray without ceasing. If we are not able to achieve this, we can at least set special times for prayer each day. At these designated moments, we can focus entirely on God.
>
> Here are some natural opportunities: when we wake in the morning; before we begin our work; before and after meals; when we go to bed.
>
> This is only a start, of course. We should not think of these times of prayer as a ritual. Neither do they mean we are freed from prayer at other times of the day. Think of these as nothing more and nothing less than a discipline for your spiritual weakness. It is a stimulation for your groggy soul. There will be times when you are under stress, times when you will be aware of others in difficulty. Immediately turn to God in prayer. Offer prayers of thanks all through the day.

When you pray, do not put any limits on God. It is not your business to tell God how to answer your prayers. This is not a time to bargain or set conditions. Before you tell God what you want or need, ask that His will be done. This makes your will subordinate to His.[2]

You cannot, of course, actually put limits on God. What you are in danger of doing is making your concept of Him smaller than His reality. He is bigger, more powerful, more loving, and more righteous than we can imagine, so some of that is inevitable. It can be kept at a minimum by a constant awareness of our tendency to limit our prayers. There are some more great quotes on prayer at the end of chapter. I think you'll be blessed by reading them.

Method Two: Think

Remember the lesson from chapter five: God didn't give us brains just to keep our skulls from collapsing. You have the capacity to pull back and look at least somewhat objectively at your own actions, emotions, reactions, and proposed actions.

Think about what you hope to gain or achieve by what you are about to do. Is it the praise of others? Keep in mind the section of the Sermon on the Mount I talked about earlier. Jesus said that if you do good things only to receive the praise of men then that praise would be your only reward.

Is it material gain? That's not necessarily a bad thing. Everybody has to make a living. Paul sewed tents to pay his own way on his missionary journeys. But hold the gain up against the loss. If you're in debt, your kids are in school, and you are offered a part-time job that would put your family in the black in a year or so, not taking it would probably have a glimmer of that old bugaboo laziness about it. But if you realize that you're about to leave your preschoolers in daycare or your husband eating a TV dinner all alone so that you can get a bigger house, newer furniture, or a fancier vacation ...you get the point. You can figure a lot of this motivation stuff out for yourself if you just stop to think before you jump in.

Method Three: Seek Wise Counsel

After praying and using your brain, the next step is to ask for advice from someone wiser than you. Notice please that I did not say 'ask your "ditsiest" friend what to do.' Find a more experienced Christian brother or sister and ask if they see any flaws in your reasoning so far. Ask them to pray for you as you make this decision.

Method Four: Check Scripture

Keep in mind that nothing God reveals to you in some other way will ever contradict His written Word. If it does, then it isn't from God but some other source: the world, your fallen nature, or the devil.

Something may be telling you to eat the *whole* lemon meringue pie. It isn't God. Something may be telling you to buy the "Abdicator" or the five-point diamond tiara from QVC. It isn't God.

You may have a very real urge to tell your friend, your husband, or the pastor what the Lord has revealed to you is wrong with them. The urge didn't come from God.

But I Thought …

This brings us to the first common misconception, which is that if God has given you insight and discernment into how someone else is going wrong, He did it so you could run and tell them about it. Blaaaat! Wrong answer! He did it so you could pray for them.

All that discernment and wisdom God has poured into you as you read the Bible, studied the books of great teachers, and prayed was given for application in your own life but only for prayer in the lives of others.

Another common misconception is that you can do wrong for the right reason and still be acting within God's will because, after all, He judges the heart. Hate to disillusion you, but unless you had no idea that what you were doing was wrong, that philosophy isn't going to cut any mustard with God. Of course He'll forgive you, but there is that heart-wrenching repentance phase to go through. All the passages about God being faithful to forgive our sins have an "if" in them: 'If you confess, and are heartily sorry . ..'

The first time the baby colors on the wall she does it just because she wants to see the pretty colors. Unless her mother is so permissive she's almost unconscious, every time after that it's disobedience. God doesn't honor disobedience.

The last common misconception is that if you know you are right you should let nothing stop you. Lots of things should still be able to stop you.

When my friend, Carol Anderson, was new to the job of being a pastor's wife, she got into a disagreement with the president of the United Methodist Women at her church. Carol knew she was right, and she argued the woman into submission, using Scripture. When she got home, she told her husband about it, blow for blow, feeling very proud of herself. When she asked what he thought, he said, "I think you won the fight and lost the friend." Even if you're right, it's wrong to trample on people's feelings. That should stop you.

There's also the story about a woman who had a green light at an intersection near my home. She went ahead without looking to the right or left and an eighteen-wheeler smashed her to smithereens. No one knows if he was running the light, didn't see the light, or was asleep at the wheel. It doesn't really matter now; they're both dead. That woman was in the "right"—she was dead right.

The point of telling this true story is to illustrate the fact that timing is important. The proposed action may be right, but we are well advised to seek God's timing. Ecclesiastes 8:5b–6 says, "the mind of a wise man will know the time and the way. For every matter has its time and way, although man's trouble lies heavy upon him."

My prayer for myself and for you is: "Father, search our hearts. We know we stand perfect in Your sight, covered by faith in the righteousness of Jesus, but we want to grow more and more like Him. Show us the places where we've been fooling ourselves. Help us turn away from pride, greed, lust, laziness, vengeance, and despair and toward You, trusting You to help us grow. We pray in Jesus' name. Amen."

QUOTES ON PRAYER

- **Evagrius Ponticus, 345–399, A.D.:** "It is a mistake to ask God to give you what you want. Your desires are probably not in complete harmony with God's will. Pray instead that God will lead you to want the right things. Ask for what is good and best for your soul"[2]

- **Walter Hilton, 1343–1396 A.D.:** "When you pray, intend to make your prayer as complete and honest as you can. If you are dissatisfied with the results of your effort, do not be too angry with yourself. Do not complain that God has not given you the kind of devotion he gives to others. Instead, acknowledge your weakness, consider it a valid prayer, and trust that in his mercy, God will make it good. Do your part and allow our Lord to give you what he will. You are not praying in order to teach God anything"[2].

- **Francis de Sales, 1567–1622 A.D.:** "Make frequent, short little prayers to God. Express your appreciation for His beauty. Ask Him to help you. Fall at the foot of the cross. Love His goodness. Give your soul to Him a thousand times a day. Stretch out your hand to Him like a child. If such prayerful, intimate thoughts become habitual, you will gain a beautiful familiarity with God.

When you really love God, you won't be able to stop thinking about Him"[2].

• **Bernard of Claivaux, 1090–1153 A.D.:** "If you want to pray, you must choose not only the right place, but also the right time. Quiet time is best. The deep silence when others are asleep inspires natural prayer. Prayer is a secret thing at night. It is witnessed only by God"[2].

DISCUSSION QUESTIONS

1. When are you most tempted to brag? (Penny's answer: about children and grandchildren.)

   _____

   _____

   _____

   _____

   _____

2. Can you think of other biblical stories where bragging played a part?

   _____

   _____

   _____

   _____

   _____

3. Talk about the "lie" verses the "gold." Can you think of ways to dislodge the lie from your mind without giving up the gold?

   _____

   _____

   _____

   _____

   _____

4. Which unworthy motive (pride, greed, laziness, despair) do you struggle most with? Any victories to share?

_____

_____

_____

_____

_____

5. Which method for checking your motivation (praying, seeking counsel, checking Scripture, thinking) do you most often skip over? How might that mess up your decision making?

_____

_____

_____

_____

_____

6. Take a minute to reread the quotes on prayer at the end of this chapter. Which one is most meaningful to you? Why?

_____

_____

_____

_____

_____

CHAPTER 7

Don't Let the Small Stuff Spoil Your Joy

The starting point for all these lessons was the Book of Esther. However, the name of this book is not *Detailed Analysis of the History, Timelines, and Archeological Evidence Regarding the Book of Esther* but *Life lessons from Esther*. So, sometimes I started at a part of Esther that sparked a train of thought and then wandered through the Bible, trying to clarify the concept and bring it into focus. That's how this chapter will be.

As I've said, these are "how-to" lessons not salvation lessons. Salvation can only be found at the foot of the cross in the finished work of Jesus Christ. This is just about how to live within the context of that salvation.

I started thinking about not letting little things get you down as I watched Haman leaving the first banquet that Esther threw for him and the king. "And Haman went out that day joyful and glad of heart. But when Haman saw Mordecai in the king's gate, that he neither rose nor trembled before him, he was filled with wrath against Mordecai" (5:1). He started as a happy camper. Good things were happening, but as he left, he saw Mordecai, and it was all spoiled for him.

My daughter-in-law, Kelly, tells a funny story about herself and her sisters. They were maybe seven, nine, and eleven and were playing with the family video camera. They had it all rehearsed and were singing along to a record of *Annie*, all doing the same motions. Can't you just see it? The camera was rolling and they were doing great, when all of a sudden, the record stuck. Kelly and Becky kept right on going, turning on a dime to change MTV into *Saturday Night Live*, but Brandy collapsed into a heap, crying, "It's ruined; it's all ruined." Poor Brandy; it's all on tape and she will never live it down.

I'm reminded too, of a child whose whole enjoyment of a trip to the fair can be ruined if Daddy doesn't spring for cotton candy. It seems the extreme versions of this problem are often an indication of immaturity, just not being tall enough yet to see beyond a minor flaw to the very pleasant big picture.

But we are all subject to it in some degree, and we will always be better for recognizing it and rising above it.

We can try to understand where Haman was coming from. We can try to think about his life: raised as an Agagite, hating Jews. We can realize that he was probably wary of Mordecai's talents and abilities as a possible threat to his own job. Mordecai handled an exalted position well enough to be mentioned in the secular records, so he must have been an able man. Whatever extenuating circumstances Haman found himself in, it doesn't change the fact that he got hung because he made no effort to rise above them.

If we insist on concentrating on one or two flaws in an otherwise great picture, we can get flopped into a mess, just like Haman did.

Nuts And Bolts

With one exception, I decided on the topics for this series of lessons by praying for guidance, then going through the notes I had made as I studied Esther with my friend, Beverly. I underlined what seemed to me to be "life-lesson-type" points. So I had this list of lesson names, and I put one at the top of each successive page of a notebook, so that as I came across a good reference or idea in the Bible or elsewhere, I could jot it down under the appropriate topic. I worked at filling the notebook for about six months.

Then, beginning at lesson one—faithfulness I started writing, continuing to jot down ideas for the other lessons as I thought of them. When it came time to start writing this one, I was horrified to find that the page was still blank. I thought, "Maybe the title says it all. What if there is nowhere to go with this lesson?"

But I had just been reading Isaiah 50:5, where he says: "The Lord God has opened my ear, and I was not rebellious, I turned not backward". So I thought, "I'm sure this whole study has been led by God, and I prayed before I selected the topics, so why would God give me a topic where everything there is to say is self evident in the title?"

I prayed again and opened the notebook to stare at the empty page, hoping for inspiration. The first thing I saw was that the page was not *totally* empty—the title was there. That would have to be my starting point. There seemed to be three elements to the sentence.

The first was "don't let." That indicated a choice to take the initiative, an act of the will. Then came "the small stuff." What exactly was the small stuff, and where is the line drawn between big stuff and small stuff? Finally, there's "your joy." That seemed to be at the heart of what was being said.

That's how I will proceed, only backwards. I'll start by exploring and defining joy, move on to what constitutes small stuff, and finish by looking at the choice—the act of the will that's necessary to rise above circumstances, seeing over the minor irritations, and keeping your eye on the big picture.

What Joy? Where?

C. S. Lewis wrote a book called, *Surprised by Joy*. If people who only know him from the movie, *Shadowlands*, saw that, they might assume it was written about his wife, whose name was Joy, but it is the marvelous story of his conversion to Christianity. Anyone who has read it, will recognize, as I go on, that I am not defining joy in quite the way he does. What his joy and mine have in common is the fact that both are ultimately realized only in relationship to the God who is really there. Lewis' joy is a rarefied and transient transporting emotion. Mine is a nearly continual bubbling at the base of the soul of a fountain of living water that can wash everything else in there, making it clean and endurable.

Psalm 100 comes pretty close to expressing it.

Make a joyful noise unto the Lord, all the lands,
Serve the Lord with gladness!
Come into His presence with thanksgiving.

Know that the Lord is God!
It is He that made us, and we are His.
Enter his gates with thanksgiving,
And his courts with praise.
Give thanks to him—bless his name!
For the Lord is good.
His steadfast Love endures forever.

That says almost everything about the source of my joy. God is *God*. He is our Creator. Look around you. How beyond our comprehension is the one who threw the stars across the sky like confetti in a New York parade? He thought up so many kinds of plants that nobody's even been able to count them all. He wove His creation into such an intricate web that every bit of it is interconnected. The great tapestries of the Middle Ages—wonders of color and workmanship are like a two-year-old's finger painting in comparison.

He continues to sustain us because we are His. He provides the pastures that feed us. It would all fall apart without His thought under-girding it.

He is good. He isn't just there, He is *good*. He is righteous beyond our ability to understand. Most of us are still struggling along with the idea that things are supposed to be "fair." I hope I'm not the first one to break this to you, but life really isn't fair. It's not fair that some children are born smart and beautiful while others are just smart. How fair is it that some are beautiful but not too bright and some of the poor little guys are stupid and ugly? We live in a fallen world. Get used to it.

You may think I've lost all track of the fact that I'm supposed to be talking about joy. No, because who besides their parents loves the stupid, ugly ones? God does! And it applies across the board—to everybody.

He loves all of us and sets only one prerequisite for salvation, which applies to all: love God with all your heart, accept Jesus as your savior. That's just. There are no special rules for the rural Christian as opposed to the urban one. There's no difference between what smart and stupid people have to do. The same rules apply to everybody. And there is, when you get to the core of it, really only one rule for how to live: trust Me and do the very best you can with what I've given you.

This is epitomized in the parable of the talents. The master gave three guys three different amounts of money and told them to take care of it while he was gone. They didn't all get the same amount. When the master came back, the guy who only had a little hadn't even tried to use it well. He buried it. He got no reward. He wasn't expected to make as much as the guy with ten talents was, but he was expected to make *something*. God is not fair by the human definition of that word, but He is just. He doesn't care if you trust Jesus with the simple faith of a mentally challenged child or with a thoughtful, clearly comprehended theology. He just expects you to make the most of what you've been given.

What joy this all is to me. God is really there; He made us and provides for us. He is incomprehensibly righteous, and He loves me. Think of that! The God of the Universe, the God of the angel armies, the eternal, unsearchable Almighty Creator of all that is loves *me*!

He loves me so much that if I were the only one who needed to be saved, He would still have died for me. If you were the only one that needed to be saved, He would have died for you. What a depth of joy there should be for us in that knowledge. Isaiah 12:2 says:

> Behold, God is my salvation:
> I will trust and not be afraid.
> For the Lord God is my strength and my song,
> And He has become my salvation.

And it's not going to change! His steadfast love endures forever and His faithfulness to all generations. It's sure. It's solid. You can count on it. In a world where it is true to say that the only thing that doesn't change is the fact that everything changes, this is the one thing that won't!

You're not only saved, you're safe! Maybe not from the slings and arrows of outrageous fortune but from being separated from the love of God. As Romans 8:38 and 39 says, "neither death, nor life, nor angels, nor principalities, nor things present, nor things to come, nor powers, nor height, nor depth, nor anything else in all creation, will be able to separate us from the love of God in Jesus Christ, our Lord."

Seven Streams of Joy

What I just described is the only true source of joy. But it's like a mountain spring that from just one source trickles away down the hill in different streams. I've identified seven that I've experienced. I'm sure there are more.

Stream One: the Joy of Worship

The first one is the joy of worship. Remember David's song, "I was glad when they said unto me let us go into the house of the Lord" (Psalm 122:1)? The act of corporate worship and the remembrance of corporate worship and the anticipation of corporate worship can be great sources of joy. At the very end of his book, Dr. Luke tells us what happened after Jesus was carried up into heaven. He says that the apostles "returned to Jerusalem with joy, and were continually in the temple blessing God" (Luke 24:52).

Offering worship to God is a definite joy, but it doesn't have to be corporate worship. You can do it all alone or in very small groups. God says that where two or three are gathered together in His name there will He be in the midst of them.

Remember when Paul and Silas got thrown into jail? (The story is in Acts 16:19–25.) Paul had cast a spirit of divination out of a slave girl and her owners accused them of disturbing the peace. The crowd roughed them up pretty good, then the magistrates finished the job by beating them with rods and turning them over to the jailer, who threw them in a cell and clamped stocks on their feet.

Nothing is mentioned about a shower, supper, an aspirin, or a call to their attorney. Yet, in the next sentence we are told that around midnight Paul and Silas were praying and singing hymns, and the prisoners were listening to them. They didn't let uncomfortable circumstances spoil the joy they got from worshiping God with prayer and singing.

For me, singing has always been an important part of worship, and I can't really sing. Sometimes it sounds like I can, but that is an audio illusion! If you sing alongside me long enough, it will eventually dawn on you that I hit a fair number of wrong notes, and that I have the amazing ability to change keys in the middle of song and never know it. But dag-nab if I'm gonna let those little details spoil my pleasure in making a joyful noise unto the Lord!

While singing and music are pretty universal, they don't have to be part of worship. There are as many ways to worship as there are people who love God. Don't let circumstances keep you from the joy of worship.

Stream Two: Answered Prayer

I'm sure you've all experienced answered prayer of some sort. I think one reason we don't experience it more often is that we're always looking for the answer to be "sure" and to look pretty much like the request.

But that's not the way God works. He's not a short-order cook at the back of a diner, standing there waiting to deliver our eggs just the way we want them. I picture Him more like a kindergarten teacher with an agenda the kids know nothing about. If a child's request fits the agenda, it may well be granted.

"Miss Blake, can I change the calendar today?"

"Yes, Billy, it's your turn."

Sometimes the answer is "later," as in: "Miss Blake, will you read us some more of that story?"

"Later, Billy, after snack time."

Consider this: "Miss Blake, will you send Thomas home? He's bothering me!" Billy's probably going to get a "no" on that one.

A popular saying has it that God answers prayers three ways: yes, no, and later. These sayings get to be so familiar because a lot of people have recognized the truth in them and repeated them to someone else. I would add a fourth way that He answers prayer: "No, but …"

C. S. Lewis spent a lot of time in one of his books speculating about what heaven would be like. Then he said he didn't really know, of course, but that if what he had speculated wasn't true, something better would be. Sometimes our vision, and therefore our prayer, is very limited. God *could* give us what we're asking for, but He has something much better in mind.

It was many, many years before I saw the blessing in my obedience to an answer of "no, but …" At the time, I couldn't even hear the "but." I was a senior in high school, heading to Missouri University the next fall. I wanted, above all things, to study forestry or agriculture. The guidance counselors weren't having any of that—I was a girl. But the real obstacle was my mother. She had her heart set on my majoring in journalism. The "J" school at Mizzou was one of the best in the nation. I had been editor of the high school newspaper, and all the teachers praised my writing ability. Besides which, that is what Mama had wanted to do.

One Sunday morning in church, I decided, quite uncharacteristically, to pray about it. I was seventeen. I knew nothing about the way God often speaks through Scripture, and I had blessed little of it stored in my heart for Him to work with. I was praying for God to change my mother's mind and clear the way before me into the "ag" school.

Clearly—not quite audibly but clearly—there came into my mind something totally unexpected. God said, "Honor your father and your mother." Somehow, I recognized the source of this directive, and, even more astonishingly, I was obedient. From that point on, I dropped my campaign to study agriculture and went off submissively to major in journalism. It didn't seem to work out all that well in the short run. Two years later, I was kicked out of MU.

But (*now* I can hear the "but"), the Lord has used the skills I honed in those two years. Additionally, the only way I ever would have met my husband John was to get kicked out in time to get a lifeguard job at the Ramada Inn they hire in March and I never would have been kicked out if I had been hanging around with the steady, reliable types in the ag school.

From here, I can see that I wound up with a wonderful husband and the great joy of running my own small nursery for fifteen years. There I had the privilege of telling many people about the wonders of God's world. Looking back, I can see that the guidance counselors may have been "wrongheaded," but they were right. At that time, no one would have hired a woman to be a forest ranger. The best way for God to use my love of His creation was another path altogether.

At times, we actually get to catch a glimpse God's hand weaving the colored bits together to make an amazing picture. Watch for prayers to be answered in unexpected ways. Greet the answer joyfully, and for heaven's sake, write it down.

Stream Three: Things to Come

Another stream from the source of joy is the wonderful knowledge of promises as yet unfulfilled. God has given us many promises in His Word. There have been whole books written just to list God's promises. Some of those promises have not yet been fulfilled. That means they're still coming!

God has promised that He has a plan for your life, a plan for good and not for evil. If you have given Him your life and are walking along holding His hand, you can be sure your future doesn't hold *just* bad stuff. It will certainly be there, we live in a fallen world, but there will also be some wonderful things. Count on it! Look for it! Get one of those books of Bible promises or just start listing them yourself as you read the Bible. They are a source of joyful anticipation. The small, bad thing happening today has little chance of getting you down if your eyes are on God's promises for the future. Just make sure you know to whom the promise was made. Not all biblical promises are promises to you.

Fourth Stream: How Good and Pleasant It Is …

A fourth source of joy for me is brothers and sisters in Christ. No friendship is so deep and rewarding as one based on a mutual love of Jesus.

One summer, near the end of a mass-mentoring session that our women's ministry, called WOW (Women of Wisdom), I wrote this in my journal:

"I was starting to pray this morning—fourth start, having trouble concentrating—so this time I started with the Lord's prayer, and at the very first word, "Our," I thought of the little book from church camp so long ago that explained how that one little word created a brotherhood of believers worldwide.

"I had always thought of believers in China and Africa and Russia. But this morning, I thought of all the women I have shared teaching duties with in the WOW program, and it dawned on me that I have what I have always wanted: I am no longer an only child. I have sisters. As I became aware of each one as a devoted and beloved child of "my" Father, a great peace settled on my spirit. I truly have sisters. They would come if I needed them. They will pray if I ask them. They laugh at my stupid jokes. Like sisters of the flesh, we will sometimes disagree, but because we are all seeking God's will, and because the underlying bond is so permanent it can't be broken, we will always smooth it over. We are sisters in Christ. Thank You, Lord."

That was a really eye-opening moment for me. The blessing and the joy of this fellowship are so rewarding, because I know that when we have all run the race that's set before us, when we have fought the good fight, grown old, and gone home, there will be all the time in the world to laugh and talk and praise God together.

Fifth Stream: the Living Word

The fifth element I identified is God's Word. This is a joy that grows. It just keeps getting better. God's Word really is living. The more you read and study it, the more meaningful it becomes. I had read the Book of Ezekiel three times—once each year as I read through the Bible—gritting my teeth and being obedient, until all of a sudden, I *got* it. Old

"Zeke" saw something so incredible that when he tried to put it into words it just sounded crazy and stupid. God's glory and power translate poorly into the dingy language of a fallen people. This part of God's Word had (finally) given me a new dimension of understanding about whom God is. Isaiah 40:8 again: "The grass withers, and the flower fades, but the word of the Lord lasts forever."

The chapter in Lee Stroebel's, *The Case for Christ*,[3] in which he interviewed Dr. Bruce Metzger about the reliability of Scripture amazed me. I had trusted in the reliability of the Bible for a long time before I read that chapter, but was it great to have so much ammunition to use with people who didn't. I highly recommend buying this book.

I learned that what the New Testament has in its favor, especially when compared with other ancient writings, is the unprecedented multiplicity of copies that have survived from a date remarkably close to the writing of the original. Whereas the earliest surviving copies of most ancient texts (like Tacitus, the Roman historian, or Homer's *Iliad*) date eight hundred to a thousand years from the writing of the original, we have copies of the New Testament written within two or three generations of the original.

And the number of surviving ancient copies will really impress you. Consider Tacitus, who is widely cited and trusted implicitly in scholarly circles. His first six books survive on only one manuscript from about 850 A.D.; the rest of his work is in just one more manuscript from the eleventh century, and three of his books, which we know existed from other references, have been lost completely.

There are fewer than 650 manuscripts of the Homer's *Iliad*, all from the second or third century—over a thousand years after it was written! That certainly sounds better than Tacitus, and Homer is second only to the Bible in good, early manuscripts. Want to know how close a second? There are less than 650 *Iliads* but more than five thousand New Testaments, some from within two centuries after the writing of the originals!

The Case for Christ is a fine book with which to re-enforce your own faith and an invaluable evangelism tool. You do have to trust that the Bible is the inspired Word of God before you can reap its many rewards, and Stroebel's book will help you if you are having any trouble there. But you can't stop at trusting it, you also have to read it, and that is where the real joy of the Word is. Try reading these passages aloud.

Isaiah 61:1-3a:
The Lord has anointed me to bring good tidings
to the afflicted;

he has sent me to bind up the broken-hearted,
To proclaim liberty to the captives, and the opening of the prison
to those who are bound;
to proclaim the year of the Lord's favor,
and the day of vengeance of our God;
to comfort all who mourn;
to grant to those who mourn in Zion
to give them a garland instead of ashes,
and the oil of joy for mourning.

Matthew 6:19-20
"Do not lay up for yourselves treasures on earth, where moth and rust consume and where thieves break in and steal, but lay up for yourselves treasure in heaven, where neither moth nor rust consumes, and where thieves do not break in and steal. For where your treasure is, there will your heart be also."

John 14:1-2
"Let not your hearts be troubled: believe in God, believe also in me. In my father's house are many rooms. If it were not so, would I have told you that I go to prepare a place for you?"

King David said, " if I had cherished my iniquity in my heart, the Lord would not have listened". God highlighted that for me a few years ago. Have you ever seen God's "highlighter?" For me, it is often just that, as I read, a deeper meaning is revealed, but sometimes it really seems like a highlighter. In the movie, *A Beautiful Mind*, letters and numbers seemed to suddenly glow or have a light behind them for Mr. Nash. It's kind of like that, only not so Hollywood-bright, and it doesn't jump around, 'cause most of us aren't schizophrenic. Just this one thing: you'll suddenly not be able to take your eyes off of or tear your thoughts away from.

The words, "cherished my iniquity in my heart," just jumped off the page at me, and I realized that there was indeed a sin that I cherished in my heart—sort of remembered fondly—even though I had repented of it and didn't do it any more. God used His "highlighter" to help me get rid of that feeling, and that was a joy to me. The Word of God fits into your life. It illuminates you. It strengthens you. It feeds you, and when you are fed, you grow.

Sixth Stream: Every Day in Every Way

And that brings us to the sixth stream of joy: the certain knowledge that the Holy Spirit is working in your life, molding and making you into a new creation, from a seed to a flower. Growth is joy, uncomfortable joy occasionally, but joy.

Seventh Stream: the Work of Your Hands

Finally, there is the joy of all kinds of work well done. It can be what you do to make a living, what you do to make a home, or what you do to serve God. We're supposed to do each thing as unto to the Lord, and when we do it well, there is great satisfaction. Dueteronomy16:15 says, in part, "The Lord your God will bless you in all your produce, and in all the work of your hands, so that you will be altogether joyful."

Those are the seven streams of joy I was able to identify, and they are all fed by the same bubbling spring: the joy of salvation.

So What is the Small stuff?

At one particularly difficult time in my life, I came up with a bottom-line question with which to put things in perspective. It seemed like pow! pow! pow! One earth-shattering disaster after another hit me, so I started asking myself each time a new one landed, "Will this affect my salvation?" The answer of course was always no.

That got things into perspective. Naturally, I still had to figure out how to deal with the problems, and they weren't small. I had learned not to let little things spoil my joy long before. Now I had to learn not to let the big ones obliterate it either.

These couldn't be overlooked and ignored, but I could make sure the worry, care, grieving, and dealing didn't take up *all* the space in my heart. It was possible for it to coexist with joy.

You can see I'm sure, how a question that can put major disasters in perspective ought to work wonders on small stuff. So what are some of the small things?

Let It Go!

One of those things is the past. You've learned what you could from it, it's over; you can't change it now, so let it go. I'm sure you've all had the maddening experience of thinking of exactly what you should have said way too late to say it. Well, what if you just kept dwelling on it, polishing and refining that perfect but now useless comeback? How much of your real, going-on-right-now life would you miss out on?

In Philippians 3:13 Paul says, "But one thing I do, forgetting what lies behind, and straining forward to what lies ahead, I press on toward the goal for the prize of the upward call of God in Christ Jesus."

Does the past affect your salvation? No. Nothing you have done is too bad for God to forgive, if you have repented, and nothing good you accomplish can get you into heaven. Having one foot in the past, either guiltily or proudly, makes it impossible to move effectively into the future.

Blooming In Rocky Soil

Another small thing, although it doesn't always seem like it, is the circumstances of your life. You probably didn't plan when you were sixteen on being where you are today. You may have thought you'd have four or five kids, and the Lord hasn't seen fit to give you any. You may have thought you'd be climbing the corporate ladder, and instead you're home with babies. You may have pictured that at this stage of your life you'd be comfortably retired and enjoying the pleasures of being called Grandma, but you still need to work, and your children are all on the "pill" and living in sin. You may have never wanted to leave a job you loved, but your body wimped out on you and you are forcibly retired.

Me, I wanted land so badly! I wanted to live in the middle of a thousand acres and never see my neighbor's smoke. I wanted to drive a tractor and dig in the dirt all day long. Instead, for fifteen years I raised kids in a suburban house in Bowie, Maryland. And I did let that spoil my joy for a while. It finally dawned on me that I was cutting off my nose to spite my face. This was what I had. There were a lot of good things about it, and if I chose not to enjoy them, that was nobody's fault but my own.

Blooming where you're planted is another old saw that is very good advice. I read a book a long time ago, set in the Middle Ages. One of the characters was a priest who felt blessed by his great wealth. He had a hut of his own in the woods with a loft for his bed. That left room below for what he felt to be an inordinate luxury—he owned a comfortable chair and three books. He hoped someday to own a fourth book, but he didn't let that spoil his pleasure in what he already had.

You can certainly work to change the circumstances of your life, but don't fail to enjoy what you have in the meantime.

Don't Keep Busy

Another truly small thing that has occasionally spoiled my joy, and has often come close to spoiling it, is my "to-do" list. Half the time I make it and then lose it, wasting a couple of hours trying to find it. Or else I forget I made it until it's too late to get any of it done.

I'm not talking about a list that says, "pray, study the Bible, make time to play with the kids, call my sick friend, kiss Johny more, try a new recipe, putter around in the garden." If those were the things on my list, I can guarantee, it wouldn't have gotten lost. I'm talking about the list that says things like "clean out the hall closet, scrub the dining room floor, pick up the dry cleaning, edge the driveway, shop for new curtains." We need to learn to tell the difference between the seemingly urgent and the truly important.

My laundry room curtains fell apart in the wash a few years ago. Getting new ones stayed at the bottom of my list so long, I finally decided that the laundry room, which is on the north side of the house, got more light without curtains, and that it looked just fine the way it was. Someday, I'll take down the little brackets that held the rods, and then it will look even better. I have scratched those curtains off the list.

There are so many things, which are very small stuff, that we allow to have power over us. If you have children and do a great job raising them, or if you teach Sunday school and really convey the concept of God's love to your students, or if you are an artist or a writer and give that your best effort, or if, as a social worker, you turn a number of seemingly lost lives around—the list could go on and on—all of those things could still be having ripple effects a hundred years from now.

In a hundred years nobody will even know, let alone care, that I didn't have curtains in my laundry room. That is another question that will help you differentiate the big from the small: "What difference will it make in a hundred years?"

Choose Life

It's important to get this straight in your mind and choose to let go of the small stuff. The first thing to remember is that it *is* a choice, and you're the only one who can make it. God told the people of Israel as they entered the Promised Land that He put before them that day blessing and cursing, life and death, and He advised them to choose life.

I once had to deal with a family member who was a very angry person. Every frustration was dealt with by getting angry about it—usually at me. Finally, in the very midst of one of these bouts of anger, I said calmly, "Look, I didn't do what you say I did, and you thinking it doesn't make it true. You can be mad if you want to. You can raise your blood pressure and shorten your life over this kind of thing, but I'm not going to play the game any more. I'm not mad at you, and I'm going to treat you as if you weren't mad at me. What you do is up to you." Then I chose to leave that mess behind me and not look back. Not the person—the mess. Remember, it's a choice, and its *your* choice.

What's So Funny?

We are! For me the most effective method of getting things back in perspective is humor. If you can get up high enough to look down and see yourself through God's eyes, it will be pretty funny. Once you can laugh at yourself, you're halfway home to getting it all in perspective. Don't think God doesn't have a sense of humor. That picture of the guy with a log in his eye trying to do delicate speck-removal surgery on his brother's eye is one of the funniest visual gags I've ever seen.

One of the reasons we laugh at comedians is that they put the situations of our lives in perspective. We laugh at the unexpected little paradigm shifts. To see something that seemed dead serious a minute ago, now in a funny light, is very unexpected. If we can get a God's eye view, much of our angst becomes hilarious. Save your anger for the things that make God angry. Don't use it up on the neighbor who never brings in her garbage can. Save your grief for real loss. Don't waste it on dreams you never even really pursued. I had a young friend who wasted a number of years grieving over the fact that her mother hadn't let her try to be a model. Even if that had been a doable dream (which it wasn't), it was water under the bridge. Move on.

Climb Out of The Clutter

Use those questions: "Will this affect my salvation?" "What difference will it make in a hundred years?" Use humor, remembering it's a choice. Finally, apply the principles of Philippians 4:8. It says that whatever is true, pure, lovely, gracious, honorable, praiseworthy, just, or excellent is what you should think about. Turn your focus away from the trivial and tawdry toward the beautiful and true.

Keeping your mind on what is true involves recognizing what is speculation. For instance, if someone says something that has several possible interpretations, do you have a tendency to believe the most hurtful one? Concentrate on what is true. You do not *know* how they meant it.

If your fourth grader is struggling with long division, don't build a disaster in your mind, like the thought, "She'll never get into college." Concentrate on what's true: she needs help with long division.

If someone drops by to bring you something on a day when your house is a little messy, don't grab the delivery and keep yourself firmly planted in the doorway, assuming that if she comes in right now and sees the mess, she will never like you again. Concentrate on what's true: Here is an opportunity to show hospitality, to make some one feel valued and appreciated. If she judges you because there are some newspapers and toys on the floor and some dishes in the sink, she's not living in the real world.

Dwelling on what is praiseworthy and excellent is also a good way to avoid being judgmental. Every time a flaw in someone else comes to your mind, remember the Golden Rule, from Matthew 7:12:

"Do unto others as you would have them do unto you."(my paraphrase). Isn't it your hope that your friends will value you for your virtues, instead of judging you for your faults? Not one of us is perfect. So if your friend is always late, concentrate on her generosity. If she's a gossip, concentrate on how much volunteer work she does.

And how about all those things in the middle of Philippians 4:8: lovely, pure, gracious, honorable, and just? I actually made a list of stuff like that—things that inspire or uplift me or that are beautiful—so that I could dig it out to read when my mind was trying to run to the ugly or the unjust. Here are a few items from my list and from the lists of friends.

1. *Amazing Grace* played on bagpipes
2. Corrie ten Boom's life
3. swimming underwater
4. laughing with family and friends
5. church bells on a snowy night
6. Winston Churchill rallying the English people
7. children's choirs
8. God's Word
9. seeing things through a microscope (order and design)
10. an eagle in flight

11. standing firm when outnumbered and over-run
12. watching my children do things I can't do
13. hot chocolate
14. dolphins jumping in the sea
15. the smell of freshly baked bread
16. garden dirt between my toes
17. the smell of rain
18. Handel's "Messiah"
19. snow falling
20. sunlight hitting dewdrops
21. monks in the middle ages, copying and il-luminating the Bible
22. the sound of katydids in September

Did you notice how many are very simple? These are the kinds of things God wants us to keep foremost in our minds. Make your own list and then use it.

First Things Last

Finally, of course, pray! Prayer should always be the first thing *and* the last thing. Ask for wisdom to see the small stuff. Ask for courage and humor to rise above it. Pray with Paul that you will forget what lies behind, strain forward to what lies ahead, and "press on to the goal of the prize of upward call of God in Christ Jesus."

DISCUSSION QUESTIONS

1. Which of the things the author classified as small stuff is most apt to spoil your joy?

   _____

   _____

   _____

   _____

   _____

2. Apply the questions, "Will this affect my salvation?" and "What difference will it make in a hundred years?" to a current aggravating situation. Does that change your perspective?

   _____

   _____

   _____

   _____

   _____

3. What will you do differently because of that change in perspective?

   _____

   _____

   _____

   _____

   _____

4. Can anybody share another method of adjusting his or her perspective?

_____

_____

_____

_____

_____

_____

5. Can anyone give an example of when being able to see the humor in a situation turned things around?

_____

_____

_____

_____

_____

_____

6. If you made a Philippians 4:8 list, where will you put it so that you can find it when you need it? Share some things you would put on your list.

_____

_____

_____

_____

_____

_____

CHAPTER 8

You're Where God Put You

The people of Israel, after wandering forty years in the desert, eating only manna and the occasional quail, were about to enter the land God had promised them—a land flowing with milk and honey. Moses would not be allowed to enter with them and he knew it, so he made sure he went over their whole history with them one last time.

He pointed out God's mighty deeds on their behalf, which, although they were only children at the time, they had seen for themselves. He reviewed their mistakes and their arrogance, including his own, and then he warned them not to forget in the midst of the good times ahead who had been their strength in the bad times and who put them in the good place they were about to claim. Here's what Moses said to the Israelites in Deuteronomy 8:11–18.

> Take heed lest you forget the Lord your God, by not keeping His commandments, and His ordinances and His statutes, which I commanded you this day: lest, when you have eaten and are full, and have built goodly houses and live in them, and when your herds and flocks multiply, and your silver and gold is multiplied, and all that you have is multiplied, then your heart be lifted up, and you forget the Lord your God, who brought you out of the land of Egypt, out of the house of bondage, who led you through the great and terrible wilderness, with its fiery serpents and scorpions and thirsty ground where there was no water, who brought you water out of the flinty rock, who fed you in the wilderness with manna which your fathers did not know, that He might humble you and test you, to do good in the end.
>
> Beware, lest you say in your heart, "My power and the might of my hand have gotten me this wealth." You shall remember the Lord your God, for it is He that gives you power to get wealth; that He may confirm his covenant which He swore to your fathers.

All of us Americans, through no merit or effort of our own, have been born into a land flowing with milk and honey. And we have a massive tendency to forget who put us here.

We live in a land where even the poorest people don't really need to worry about starving; the government will give them food stamps and the inner-city missions give out meals, even taking sandwiches to the homeless who won't come to the shelters for help. I'm not trying to diminish the fact that there are people in this country who need our help, just to say that, put in a global perspective, it could be a great deal worse. I once saw a sign on the back of a metro bus that said, "There are six hundred people in Washington, DC who need shelter." We should be concerned about those six hundred, but how many people do you think need shelter in Calcutta?

Why are we the lucky ones? Why don't our children have the bloated bellies of famine and malnutrition? Why do we have the luxury of worrying about being too fat?

Well, I don't know. I don't have a clue. What I do know from Luke 12:48 is that from those to whom much is given, much will be required. We are, therefore, well advised not to take it all for granted or to forget who put us here or that He had a purpose in doing it.

Who Put Her There?

My starting point for this lesson, as always, is in Esther. Here we come to what is probably the most famous line in Esther, the one that Bev and I thought would be the crux of our study when we started.

> Then Esther spoke to Hathach and gave him a message for Mordecai, saying, "All the king's servants and the people of the king's provinces know that if any man or woman goes to the king inside the inner court without being called, there is but one law: all alike are put to death, except the one to whom the king holds out the golden scepter that he may live ...and I have not been called to come in to the king these thirty days." And they told Mordecai what Esther had said. Then Mordecai told them to return answer to Esther, "Think not that in the king's palace you will escape any more than all the other Jews. For if you keep silence at such a time as this, relief and deliverance will arise for the Jews from another quarter, but you and your father's house will perish. And who knows whether you have not been brought to the kingdom for such a time as this?"
>
> —Esther 4:10–14

One translation says, "elevated to the palace," another says, "put here." All these phrases indicate that the circumstances of Esther's life were in the control of something other than her own will. There is an understood prepositional phrase. There has to be some force *by which* one is brought or elevated.

By whom was she brought here? By whom was she elevated to the palace for such a time as this?

All the translations agree on "for such a time as this," which clearly indicates a purpose behind her coming. I don't think Mordecai could have been referring to the king and his queen search. The "time" he was referring to was one where it was necessary to circumvent one of the king's edicts. Clearly, it was not the king who brought her there for that. He had an entirely different agenda.

There is a debate among liberal theologians as to whether Esther is a sacred or a secular book. The debate centers on the fact that God's name is never mentioned. It seems clear to me that Mordecai was talking about the one who would also have provided another path of deliverance for the Jews if Esther had wimped out. I know of no earthly ruler with that kind of power and authority.

We can speculate 'til the cows come home, but no one really has a clue why God chose not to have His name mentioned in the Book of Esther. It will no doubt all come clear when we are with the Lord. I have often thought that the most commonly overheard remark in heaven will be, "Well, of course. Why didn't I think of that?" We don't know now why He chose to leave His name out of it, but one thing I am sure of, it was His *choice*, not the random inclusion of a secular story in a holy book.

I believe in the God who is really there, who loves us and does not tell us lies and who did not allow anything to be included in His Word that He didn't want there or allow anything left out that He did want there. I take seriously the admonition in 1 Timothy 3:16 that all scripture is profitable for teaching and reproof.

Everyone agrees that there are sweeping themes in the Bible. The Book of Exodus teaches redemption, the Book of Job repentance, and the Book of Esther is largely about God's providence—His care for His chosen people, even when they are not acting wholly within His will. But I have never found that God tells simple stories. There are always nuggets to be mined, something new to see with each succeeding reading, layered wisdom to be unearthed.

Where to Dig for Nuggets

Christian maturity is not measured by knowledge but by character. You will know you are a grown-up Christian when you have control of your tongue, you have a compassionate heart, and you have achieved personal integrity. You remember the definition of integrity; that's where all your thoughts, opinions, attitudes, words, and actions are saying the same thing your parts are all working together.

You reach the point were you are living God's Word by first acquiring God's Word and then by acting on it. The ways of acquiring are to hear, read, study, memorize, and meditate on it. These are the parts of the familiar "hand" illustration.

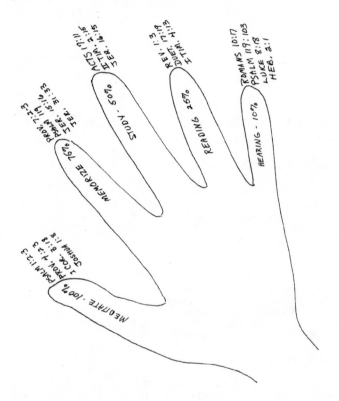

It shows how to go about getting a good grip on the Word of God through those five disciplines. It illustrates very well that you have to go beyond hearing and reading to have a solid grip on the word. Just try to pick up anything with your ring finger and pinkie.

With the last two alone (thumb and forefinger), you can actually handle it, because memorization necessarily includes either reading or hearing, and because meditation, which is thinking about, mulling over, dwelling in, and waiting on the Lord's illumination, often involves some aspects of study. It's a very good illustration.

I became sure of one thing as I continued to read, study, and meditate on the Book of Esther: whatever Mordecai's shortcomings* may have been, he knew he was a member of a chosen people whose God

---

*Maybe he would have been more in God's will if he had returned to Jerusalem with the first round of returnees as soon as Cyrus said they could go. But remember, all the people, who would later go back with Ezra, including Ezra himself, had also not gone back with the first group.

Maybe, if he saw the conscription of pretty girls coming, he should have hidden Esther in the basement or packed some bags and bugged out into the desert with her, but we aren't told if there was any warning. Perhaps the king's goons just swept out across the city and spotted Esther picking out some pomegranates in the local market. We do not have enough information to make a judgment about that.

One widely distributed commentary stated as fact (with no "maybes" or "perhapses") that Mordecai, as an employee of the king, saw these girls being brought in for the beauty contest. He thought Esther had a chance at the big prize, so he entered her. Where does he get that? Not from the Bible! It's possible that it happened that way; but judging by the way that Mordecai acts through the rest of the book, it doesn't seem likely. I have nothing against speculation, but I want to see it labeled as such and not presented as fact.

Talking about it as a beauty contest troubles me too. A lot of people use this feeble comparison. A contest is something people enter voluntarily in hopes of winning a prize. The best indication we have is that these girls had no choice in the matter. I've never heard of a pageant where the judge got to sleep with each of the girls as part of the selection process and all the losers were made into love slaves for life. Maybe it's done in an effort to make Esther a more accessible story in this day. I don't think we need to do things like that. Our Lord doesn't pull any punches. He tells the whole truth—what really happened—, the ugly along with the beautiful.

would not let them be completely eradicated. Help would arise from another quarter, he told Esther, if she wasn't up to the job.

He thought that fasting, with its corollary of prayer, was the right thing to do in an emergency. It's true that it was Esther who requested that the whole Jewish population of the city fast, but Mordecai agreed readily, and besides, where do we think she learned that if not from Mordecai? I'm pretty sure spiritual disciplines were not part of the queen training.

I believe God has lessons for us in the Book of Esther beyond an illustration of His providence. I'm sure there were any number of things that happened to the Jews in exile that would have demonstrated God's providence. This one has richness and depth. There are nuggets to be mined, truths to be found, and one of the things to be learned is that God puts people where He wants them. He has specific purposes in mind for them.

Eugene Peterson, in his introduction to the Book of Matthew in The Message, says, "Every day we wake up in the middle of something that is already going on, that has been going on a long time: genealogy, and geology, history and culture, the cosmos and God. We are neither accidental nor incidental to the story." God's purpose will prevail, even if people use their free will to dodge His draft.

The dodger will miss the blessing. God's plan will not be diverted.

It's important to remember that God put us where we are and that perhaps we were put here for such a time as this. We need to live life on purpose, meeting the challenges of each day with faithfulness and loyalty, paying attention to detail, writing down what God tells us, remembering that there are people who look to us to see what a Christian looks like, counting the cost, checking our motivation, and keeping the joy of God in our hearts, so that when the moment for which we were put here arrives (or maybe more accurately, as the moments for which we were put here continue to arrive) we will rise to the occasion, maybe without even realizing it, because acting in a godly fashion has become natural to us.

What's That Look Like?

For what kinds of purposes might we have been put here? In what ways do we affect our world? The list is endless. In addition, His ways not being our ways, there are undoubtedly purposes we fulfill that we won't even start to comprehend this side of heaven.

Let's return to "the thrilling days of yesteryear," as the radio announcer for the "Lone Ranger" used to put it. Actually, we're only going as far back as lesson four, where I talked about the movie, *It's a Wonderful Life.* I said that one of the reasons the movie continues to resonate with people was that, except for the angel part, it reflects reality.

I have said that none of us are probably where we thought we'd be at this stage of our lives. George Bailey thought he was going to travel the world on a tramp steamer, come back to attend college, and then become a reporter. I'm sure there have been many lives that have closely reflected the plot line of that movie, so let's pretend for a minute that this was a true story.

George Bailey didn't get to go where he wanted to go. One after another, he put the needs of other people ahead of his personal dreams and goals. First, he saved his brother's life, and then he laid down his own dreams so his brother could pursue his. Then his dad needed him, and then the town needed him.

We get a pretty dismal picture later in the film when we're shown what his family and his town would have been like if he hadn't been there. We even get a glimpse of the wider ripples that his life created when we're shown that if he hadn't saved his brother's life, the brother wouldn't have been there to save countless other lives with his skill as an ace pilot in the war. There would have been extra ships sunk and towns destroyed without his flying skills.

They don't project it this far in the movie, but remember the old saying: "For want of a nail, the shoe was lost. For want of a shoe, a horse was lost. For want of a horse, a knight was lost. For want of a knight, a battle was lost. For want of a battle, the war was lost. And all because of a horseshoe nail."

I'm sure there are times when ordinary people, just serving God by doing what is right, play the part of that nail. It might go something like this: "For want of little brother Bailey, an arms shipment was lost; for want of arms, a battle was lost; for want of a battle the war was lost; and all because George didn't jump in the ice-cold water."

Each time, as George laid aside his plans in service to someone else's needs, he couldn't see the big picture. And if it were real instead of a movie, he never would have—not in this life!

Once in a great while, the purpose for which you've been put where you are can be discerned, but 99.5 percent of the time, you can't see it.

I'd be willing to bet a nickel—if I were a betting woman—that during the Great Depression God had at least one George Bailey-type person in every town in America, helping, encouraging, not giving up.

We may not be able to get the big picture totally in focus, but we can get a pretty good handle on what kinds of purposes and in what sorts of ways we effect our world when we stand tall and walk in the ways

God tells us are right. I've categorized them by the ways they make their impact: ripple effect, direct effect, ricochet effect, and prayer effect.

Where Do You Have Impact?

First, let's look at two areas of impact. They are civic impact, which changes society, institutions, or culture; and personal impact, which changes an individual's life both for the current time and for eternity.

In the Bible, who besides Esther can we look to for examples of civic impact? The most striking example is probably the prophet Nathan, who called King David to account concerning his sin with Bathsheba and later had a hand in picking his successor. The last half of David's reign was troubled, as he dealt with the consequences of his sin. Can you imagine what kind of tribulation the Lord would have sent if Nathan hadn't called David to repent?

The first present-day person I thought of was Chuck Colson, who started Prison Fellowship, and has had a major impact on a number of correctional facilities. Some younger readers may not know that before he started that ministry, Mr. Colson was a highly placed member of the Nixon administration. He had a leading part in the cover up of the Watergate scandal. He went to jail. But before he went to jail, the press and the late night comedians had a grand old time lampooning him, because he made public the fact that he had accepted Jesus Christ as his Lord and Savior and was born again. They aren't laughing anymore. They are having their people call his people to see if they can book him for their show. In prison and out, he has lived by Jesus' admonition that when we visit and serve prisoners it is the same as doing it for Him.

The Reverend Martin Luther King has his own holiday now, but that is the least of his civic impact. His leadership of the civil rights movement, which he based on Christian principles, saved this country untold turmoil. It was absolutely necessary that all citizens of this country be treated equally under the law. Legalized discrimination was an abomination to the Lord, and it would have been changed one way or another. Dr. King led us along the high road of non-violence.

Consider the men and women of the ACLJ (American Center for Law and Justice) and the Rutherford Institute. Both of these organizations defend, without compensation, people whose religious rights have been violated. One case was that of a Kansas woman, an employee of the state (or the county), who posted a sign in her office that read, "In God We Trust." That phrase appears on every piece of money she handles in the course of her work, and yet the American Civil Liberties Union sued to get her to either take down the sign or be fired. Can you imagine how quickly our right to religious expression would disappear without these organizations of Christian people standing in the gap for us?

None of these high-profile people are perfect. Neither was King David. Neither are we. But if we keep turning back to God and walking in His ways, He will use us to have more impact than we will ever know. He put us right where we are for that purpose.

Civic impact can be on a local scale, too. If you take a stand against Sunday morning little league games or convince your local convenience store to put *Playboy* and *Penthouse* behind the counter, out of the sight of little eyes, you are having a definite civic impact.

The second area is personal impact. It occurred to me at this point that all impact is ultimately personal impact. If Mr. Colson manages to reform the system even partially in a certain jail, that will have a very personal impact on the people in that jail. This holds true in all the other areas of civic impact that I mentioned. The difference is that with the civic reform, the personal impact is secondhand. In personal impact, the action is one-on-one.

Think back through your life to the people who changed how you thought or how you viewed the world. Maybe a teacher held you to a higher academic standard. Perhaps a Sunday school teacher made you realize that it wasn't about religion, it was about God. There may have been a family friend or an aunt or uncle who made you feel valued and appreciated. That is personal impact, and you are having it somewhere, whether you are aware of it or not. This is the question to pose to yourself and to ask God to help you see the answer to: "Is the impact I'm having pleasing to God? Am I doing what He put me here to do, or am I wimping out on Him?"

The Reverend Billy Graham has had a personal impact on the lives of hundreds of thousands of people. My friend, Dorothea Saavedra, was saved many years ago at a Billy Graham crusade in New York. She and all the other people who have come into a personal relationship with our Lord through Mr. Graham's teaching have made a personal impact on many other people. Here we see the first way that the results of our civic or personal impact can be perceived: the ripple effect.

Ripples in the Stream

A number of years ago my daughter gave me a book to read on chaos theory. She was writing her doctoral dissertation in economics at the time, and I really think she just wanted someone to share her misery. Well, believe me, if I had tried to understand the mathematical justifications put forward for the theories in that book, there would most definitely have been two miserable Henderson women. But, having a clear perception of my shortcoming in that field, I just read the words and skipped over the numbers.

Part of what I gathered from the book was that for a long time, it was assumed that order inevitably deteriorated into chaos, and one of the things people studied to see if they could discern predictability in how order breaks down was water in a tub. When it is disturbed, it initially has predictable patterns—like ripples—but then, the turbulence hits the sides of the tub; water going in opposite directions turns back and meets again in the middle and predictability disappears.

At some point, they began to see that even in the presence of chaos and unpredictability there was discernible pattern and order. I'm sure the mathematical support for all this was very elegant, but I was more taken with some of the very elegant drawings, called fractiles.

Now don't be fooled into thinking I've actually told you very much about chaos theory, because about one-fourth of the way into the book you had to have been following the math for the words to make sense. This is just the opening act, but I thought that as far as I was able to comprehend it, it was interesting and had some application to what we are talking about.

The point is that your act of loyalty, kindness, or courage, the example you set at a critical moment, the truth you speak in love will go out like ripples to have an effect on much more than the situation you're in. Even when the discernible order of the ripples disappears, there will remain pattern and order that God can use.

One example of how actions can have a ripple effect is the "What Would Jesus Do," or WWJD, bracelets. I have no idea who made the first one, but look how the effect of it has rippled around the world. It has become a reminder to pray, a catalyst for evangelism as people ask what it is, and as clear a sign of brotherhood as was a fish symbol on a door in ancient Rome.

Your words can have a ripple effect, too. In 1611, a baby boy was born in Lorraine, France to a poor peasant couple. At eighteen, he came to know the Lord Jesus. For about thirty-five years, he was first a soldier and then a footman. At the age of fifty-five, he entered the religious community of Carmelites in Paris. He was a lay brother and lived out the rest of his life—he lived to about eighty—serving mostly in the hospital kitchen. You can find him easily on the web, just search for "Brother Lawrence." Books are still in print containing his few brief letters and the written recollections of a few people about what he said.

People came from all over Europe to talk to him about practicing the presence of God. He said to one person (who wrote down the conversation), that at first it was repugnant to him to work in the kitchen but that when he had properly resolved to do all as unto God, he began to enjoy it.

Here is a quote from one of his letters:

> It is not necessary for being with God to be always at church; we may make an oratory of our heart, wherein to retire from time to time, to converse with Him in meekness, humility, and love.

Your spoken and written words have an effect on people just like Brother Lawrence's had and are still having. Those people in turn effect other people. A few lessons back I discussed the impact your written words can have. You don't have to be a polished writer for this to happen. If you are faithful to record the insights God gives you, you can trust Him to use it. It may be rippling long after you're gone. My great-grandmother wrote a little book of poems, and I found it after my father died. What a blessing. This is one of them.

A MINUTE TOO LATE

A minute too late
And the train was gone.
Just a minute too late
But I can't get on.

A minute too late
And the kind word said
Never reaches the heart
Of the loved one dead.

A minute too late
Often causes much strife
As we go on the road
That leads us through life.

And a minute too late
And we've missed a kind word
That would have brightened our lives
Like the song of a bird

Yes, minutes are very
Important in life
For the dear little children,
The husband and wife.

In a moment in time
There's a thing can be said
That will brighten the life
Or make it feel dead.

Then let us be careful
What we do or say
That our records may show
At the close of each day,

Many kind words spoken
Many kind deeds done
Don't wait 'til too late
Or the train will be gone.

And how are we spending
Our minutes today?
Have kind words been spoken
To ease someone's way?

Or are we a minute too late?

This is not world class poetry, but it sure blessed me, and I will preserve it so that it may bless another generation of her descendants. This lady, my mother's grandmother, died long before I was born, but in reading the rest of her poems, it is clear she knew my Lord and Savior. Like this stanza:

And let us praise our great God
For the privilege that He gave
Of teaching Christ in our own home
That our children might be saved.

You do not have to appear to the world, or even to yourself, like some great saint for your words spoken or written to be used by God. You don't have to be perfect for God to use you. The woman who wrote these poems is the one who raised my grandmother, who in turn raised my mother, who felt the necessity of making a great and deliberate effort to put racism behind her. Nobody's perfect. You don't have to be perfect; you just have to be willing to be used. You have to say with Isaiah, "Here am I! Send me." (Isaiah 6:8).

Teaching can have a ripple effect, too. Take that sermon on integrity George Anderson preached in 1999. I learned from it directly. I was sitting in the pew. He could see me. He couldn't see the readers of this book, but the effect of it is still rippling as I use what I learned that day to illustrate the points I'm making. Only a small part of what I'm teaching in these lessons is original. I have been well instructed, both in my church, by radio teachers, and by current and classic writers. Their ripples are still spreading.

One on One.

The effect of your obedience can be ripples, or it can be direct. You directly effect individuals in parenting, in marriage, in evangelism, in the charitable service you perform—the very literal "feeding of His sheep" and in Good Samaritan acts. It could even be the upbeat, caring face with which you walk through life that has an impact on someone.

You can have a direct effect on institutions. The obvious way is when you vote but also when you speak up publicly against injustice or impurity. Consider Jonah. He really didn't want to go to Ninevah. The Lord had to take extreme measures to get him there. But when he finally did what God told him to do, the whole big city of Ninevah wound up in sackcloth and ashes, and their destruction was delayed because of their repentance.

You also effect institutions by participating in them. As a Girl Scout leader I noticed that the moms who complained the most about how I was running the troop were the ones who were never available to be an extra hand when we were doing a craft and never had time to be part of a carpool to some event. You don't earn the right to have an impact on how things are done until you have participated.

The Ricochet Effect

The third form of impact is the ricochet effect. It happens all the time but is most clearly illustrated in its negative aspects. You all know what a ricochet is; you fire at the intended target, but that turns out to be pretty hard and the bullet bounces off and hits something way over there. This causes a wholly unanticipated result, like the angry word fired off a spouse that hits and injures a child.

It can happen for good too. The good deed you aim at one person may get deflected or dispersed—more like a water balloon than a bullet—and impact people you never thought about. The ripples are the predictable result. The ricochet is the unpredictable chaos that follows where there is still order and pattern that God can use.

Lift It Up—The Effect of Prayer

The fourth effect is the effect of prayer. The Bible tells us that the prayers of the righteous have great power. (James 5:16). Prayer changes real stuff. I told about how I thought God honored one obedience of mine (His instruction of "honor your father and mother") and blessed me through the years when I was ignoring Him. I think another reason it happened that way was that I had two praying grandmothers: one Catholic, one Baptist. These were two godly women who I know prayed for me. They were both gone before I was ten. The effect of their prayers wasn't.

I know I have seen people healed who were given up for lost or were disabled for life through God's response to prayer. We don't change things by praying. God changes things. It's His choice what things to change. Remember my example of Billy and his kindergarten teacher? He asked to change the calendar and she said yes because it was his turn. If he hadn't asked, perhaps she would have done it herself, or maybe it wouldn't have gotten done that day. It's important to ask.

In his book, *The Prayer Matrix*, David Jeremiah says, "The biggest reason for why God asks us to pray is this: Scripture insists that God has hard-wired the universe in such a way that He works primarily through prayer. God has set up creation in such a way that He does His work through the prayers of His children. At the moment we pray, we become subject to the most powerful force in the universe"[1].

The way that prayer *always* has impact is on the person praying. As we come daily to the foot of the cross, creep shyly into the throne room, or attempt to storm the gates of heaven in our desperation, we give God the opening to work in our own hearts. We give Him the chance to give us the desires of our hearts, to change what we think we want, so that it comes in line with His character, which is always better in the long run. As that happens, we become more and more effective in all areas of our lives.

The challenge from this lesson is to think about and pray about exactly where you are in your life and what purposes God may have in mind for putting you there.

This is my prayer for all of us.

"Father, please illuminate our minds and hearts so we can see some small piece of your big picture. Weave us into it like brightly colored threads, in just the spot you want us. Use us in this time and place. We ask it in the precious name of your Son, our Lord and Savior, Jesus Christ. Amen."

DISCUSSION QUESTIONS

1. Which finger of the hand illustration is the most challenging for you?

   _____

   _____

   _____

   _____

   _____

   _____

2. What specific steps could you take to grow in that area?

   _____

   _____

   _____

   _____

   _____

   _____

3. Have you ever had a moment when you knew God wanted you to speak up?

   _____

   _____

   _____

   _____

   _____

   _____

4. Did you do it? What was the result?

_____

_____

_____

_____

_____

_____

5. Do you have areas like Penny's great-grand-mother did where your attitudes or actions are at odds with your faith?

_____

_____

_____

_____

_____

_____

6. What can you do to reclaim your integrity in that area? (Hint: confess, repent, and pray is always the best start. Where do you go from there?)

_____

_____

_____

_____

_____

_____

CHAPTER 9

So What's the Deal with Vashti?

Originally, I had planned to deal with Vashti in the first chapter (the one about loyalty), but when I started writing it, I found I didn't have enough information to come to any sound conclusions about her character or her motives, so I left her out.

One of my advisors questioned why I hadn't used Vashti as an example, and when I told her, she advised never to avoid a person, situation, or teaching in the Bible because you don't yet fully understand it. Just make sure you make that clear to the people you're teaching. So, consider yourselves warned.

Remember my theme verse from the Message version of Ephesians? "Here I am teaching and writing about things way over my head." If I felt that the rest of the lessons were over my head, then Vashti is in orbit.

Fact

I want to start by going over very carefully exactly what we *know* about Vashti. We know from Esther 1:11 that she was the queen. We know from Esther 1:15 and Esther 4:11 that the queen was not exempt from the palace rules. We know from Esther 1:11 that she was beautiful. We know from that same verse that Xerxes took pride in her beauty. We know from Esther 1:9 that while Xerxes was entertaining the important men of the kingdom Vashti was simultaneously throwing a banquet for the women. We know from Esther 1:7 that there was a lot of drinking going on at the men's banquet. We know from Esther 1:12 that when Xerxes sent seven eunuchs to order her to come to the men's banquet, she refused to come. We know that as a consequence of that refusal, she was banished from the king's presence. These are the things we absolutely know. There are also some things we can have reasonable certainty about from archeology and other ancient writings.

We can be pretty sure about why Xerxes was throwing this six-month long feast. It seems he was preparing the minds of top officials from all corners of his far-flung realm for the launching of a war to extend his territory even further. To gain their full support, he wanted to show them that his great wealth was equal to the task. It cost money to wage war then, as it does now. He also wanted them all to brainstorm and lay down a strategy.

Archeological discoveries and other ancient writings show that he did indeed launch an attack across the Mediterranean against Greece. He was the victor at the famous battle of Thermoplae but was eventually defeated and had to slink back home, leaving Greece to the Greeks. It all took about four years.

This sheds light on why Vashti's refusal to appear was such a big, hairy deal. He was trying to impress these guys with his power and authority for an important reason: he wished to rule the world, and this would be the first step. It didn't look too good that he wasn't even able to control his queen.

It was after he returned from his ill-fated grasp at world domination with his tail between his legs that he "thought of Vashti and what she had done for him" in Esther 2:1. He was probably in need of comforting. He had plenty of harem girls, but perhaps the queen had done other things for him, made special sandwiches (a la Veggie Tales), or sung to him, or mixed his evening cocktail just the way he liked it. We can't know. We can speculate, considering his defeat on the battlefield and from the fact that his staff jumped right in to instigate the queen search, that maybe he was showing signs of depression.

We know from many sources that it was taboo in the Medeo-Persian culture for women to join or even appear before men at public gatherings. It just wasn't done. There is also a possibility, maybe even a probability, that Vashti was pregnant. She is mentioned on a tablet, or a monument, or some such thing as queen mother to Artaxerxes, son and successor to Xerxes. (Sorry for the vagueness. I lost track of where I read the details. It seems fairly well known though, because a lot of people mention it.) The math is convincing; take the age of Artaxerxes noted on the tablet and subtract it from the year (also recorded), and you come pretty close to the general time frame of the six-month banquet to rally the troops. Whether she was actually pregnant, or pregnant enough to be showing at the time Xerxes called for her, we cannot be sure.

Commentaries are quite divided on the subject of Vashti. Some portray her as an almost saintly figure, willing to risk dire consequences by refusing to be lewdly displayed at the front of a banquet hall full of drunken, "good old boys." Others paint a picture of a proud, rebellious woman who publicly shamed her husband and got exactly what she deserved.

Fiction

I wish I could take a poll of my readers and find what you think. Was she a courageous saint, a rebellious shrew, or do you have no clue? (I'd also love to hear everybody's explanations of why they voted the way they did, but the best I can do is run some of *my* opinions by you, some of the things that occurred to me as possibilities as I tried to get a handle on this woman we really can't get a handle on.)

- Possibility number one: Vashti had regaled the ladies with a little too much wine, was feeling no pain, having a good time, and blew the king off without really thinking it through.
- Number two: Vashti had been feeling a little neglected and decided she would show him how it felt to be ignored. This scenario also involves her being inebriated.
- Number three: Vashti honestly didn't think it would be "proper" for her to make an appearance at the men's banquet, given the cultural norms
- Number four: Vashti was pregnant, feeling nauseous, holding fluid, and not looking all that great. Would the king even have known about this? He was sort of preoccupied with world domination.

- Number five: She was really afraid to go in there under the circumstances; this room was full of guys with such high testosterone that they wanted to rule the world.
- Number six: She was drawing a moral line in the sand. "You, sir, are asking me to do something wrong, and I won't, so there! Whatcha gonna do about it?" If this was the way it went down, I guess she found out.
- Number seven: She didn't think the king was serious. This is the "He's gotta be kidding!" plot line.
- Number eight: She thought her position as queen was an appointment for life, and she wasn't that fond of the king. (Who could blame her?) This fits the "proud and rebellious" picture.

I even went pretty far afield in my speculation. (Just spinning castles in the air, remember!) What if she had recently been rude to the head eunuch, and he plotted with the rest of them to either deliver the message wrongly or not deliver it at all. He could have just told the king she said no.

Or maybe he delivered her response wrongly. What if she actually said, "Tell my lord, his imperial excellence, that I am continually at his service, but I think perhaps he is not aware that I am carrying his firstborn child, the heir to all his endeavors, and am therefore not currently so delectable a sight for his guests as he may think. Having considered this circumstance, if my lord still feels he would be blessed by my presence, I will come at once"? But maybe all the eunuch whispered in the king's ear was, "She says no."

It seems to me that, given the little we know, all but the last of these fictions are equally probable. You may have some clever theory I've left out. We have all these ideas and possibilities, but we really don't *know* any more than we did when we started.

So is there *any*thing we can learn from this woman? Well, …maybe. The first thing that struck both my friend Bev and me when we were first studying the book was that she had publicly humiliated her husband, and that no matter what the motivation may have been, that is a very bad idea.

How Would That Look Today?

Let's put out a worst-case, present-day possibility. Let's say that in a moment of temporary insanity, you married the second biggest jerk in the world. He missed out on the first biggest jerk title because he has never been unfaithful, walked out on you, or hit you, so under God's rules of engagement for marriage, you're stuck with him. This guy never calls if he's going to be late, gives you a five-dollar book of coupons to McDonald's for Christmas, spent your joint life savings on a speed boat, has yet to show up at a little league game, change a diaper, or put any kid to bed, and thinks it's funny to shame you in public. He tells your little foibles and your big failures to his buddies as jokes and tells the pastor when he comes to call that he's too much of a man to need some imaginary God for a crutch to get through life.

Suddenly, the opportunity to turn the tables presents itself. He does something stupid. How tempting is it to throw him to the laughing hyenas he calls his friends by telling it as a big joke the next time they show up. Resist! Resist! Resist that temptation!

Jesus didn't say, "Do unto other people in like manner to what they have done unto you." He said, "Do unto others as you would *have* them do unto you" (Italics and paraphrase mine). He wants us to set the standard—to lead by example whether it looks like anybody's going to follow or not.

If we're supposed to act that way toward the second biggest jerk in the world, how much harder should we be trying to never undermine or put down a man of whom we're fond, who does his best to provide for his family and who loves his children?

This can be a pretty tricky thing, especially early in marriage when you don't yet have that much information about where his vulnerabilities lie. When John and I were dating, he admired my father's slide projector, so I got him one just like it as a wedding gift. We got married, drove to Colorado for our honeymoon, had a great time, and took lots of slides. When we got home, we took the slides and the new projector over to his brother's house to show their family our pictures. After the first couple of views, Johnny started having some trouble making it work smoothly. So, I, having run one just like it since I was twelve, stepped in and showed him what he was doing wrong.

As we finished watching the slides, had dessert, and started home, all seemed as usual. But he didn't speak to me all the way home or before work the next morning, so when he got home, I begged him to tell me what was wrong, 'cause I didn't have any idea, not even an inkling. It turned out he felt I had shamed him in front of his brother by knowing how the projector worked when he didn't. That seemed insane to me, and I put up a good defense of my actions: What kind of wife would I be if I didn't help him when I had the ability to? etc, etc. I know now that was all beside the point. His pride had been wounded and in a place where he was particularly vulnerable: in front of his older brother. It's one of those areas where men's minds are just wired differently. We have to learn about the differences and be sensitive to them and not expect them to think the way we do. We certainly want them to learn to do that for us.

Vashti didn't wound just the pride of Xerxes, she got the whole cabinet against her because they were afraid their wives would start doing stuff like that. Whatever her motive—proud, pure, or indifferent—Vashti didn't come when she was called, and that shamed the king because it was such a public occasion.

> A friend of mine once had a dog called Vashti because she would never come when she was called.

Submissive Vs Righteous

So where does a Christian woman draw the line between being respectfully submissive and standing up for what's right? Vashti may have been a wonderful woman who took a stand for decency. Chuck Swindoll sees it that way, and maybe that's the way it was. There are certainly times when respecting what God says is right should take precedence over any other obligation.

Here I am, out in orbit. I have no personal experience to draw on here because I am blessed to be married to a man who would never ask me to do anything wrong. The most decadent, wrong-minded, and perverted thing he has ever requested of me is to tell someone calling on the phone that he isn't home. You'd better believe I gave it to him with both barrels for *that* one. Within his hearing, I told the person that John couldn't come to the phone and asked if I could take a message! Really walked the narrow line between submission and truth there, didn't I?

I am fully aware that this is not an even remotely funny subject for a lot of people. Someone asked me once what a Christian woman ought to do if her husband asked her to watch pornography with him and I laughed it off. I said, "I don't really know, but I know what *I'd* do! I'd wrap him around my little finger and say, 'We don't need that stuff. Follow me, big boy!'" Looking back, it is probably a pretty good strategy, but would it work on the kind of guy who really wanted to see the pornography? I don't know because I'm not married to one. Neither is my friend Carol, but for many years, she and her husband, Pastor George Anderson, have counseled with more people in troubled marriages than they probably care to remember. They offer the following comments.

Carol Anderson: In your heart, cry out to God for deliverance for your husband from the trap of pornography. We are lifelong friends of a couple who were missionaries for twenty-five years. He got involved in looking at pornography and is now in prison for abusing a minor. He tells us that taking a few "peeks" at pornography is never enough and will eventually result in acting it out.

So it is appropriate to cry out for deliverance. Only God's Spirit can conquer this. You are not wrestling against flesh and blood but the enemy of our souls. Put on the full armor of God's Word in your spirit before you make an appeal to your husband. Do not "spout" God's Word at your husband, but appeal to him by saying things like this: "You are the one I trust to protect me from the emotional attacks of the world. I don't think I could handle this emotionally. I am fearful that it would damage my spirit and change me and therefore damage and change our relationship."

"It would put me in a different category in life. I know that what I see affects what I think and what I do. I am afraid I would begin thinking like a fallen woman, one who has been used."

"Most women struggle with self-image anyway. If my self-image is damaged, it affects the way I respond to you, emotionally, spiritually, and physically. The conscience is a very fragile thing. I want to give you the 'best' of me. This would make me feel like all I have to give you is the 'worst' of me."

George Anderson: When it comes to sex, men are visual. And therefore anything could be considered pornography if it causes sexual arousal in a person; that is, if what is being looked at is other than one's wife. For this reason, I even try to avoid lingerie ads in the newspaper.

The husband's need for arousal needs to be satisfied without compromise. Any film specifically made to turn people particularly men on will be immoral by design. Could the wife suggest a love story movie that leaves the bedroom scenes to the imagination?

I think this initiative on her part, along with the above-mentioned appeal, would go a long way toward meeting his needs for sexual arousal without violating either his own or his wife's conscience.

The husband's resort to pornography represents some problems within himself. It may represent a sense of sexual performance anxiety in him. He may have fears of inadequacy. But how is he going to tell that to his wife?

So, rather than her withdrawing in anger and disgust (the natural thing a wife might do but the very thing that will only deepen the husband's sense of inadequacy), she should take some sexual initiatives with her husband. This will have the effect of both helping his sense of inadequacy and distracting his attention from the pornography.

A man who wants to be a strong and godly man should tenaciously guard himself from pornography because it can simply ruin him, robbing him of his God-given manliness. If a man has become addicted to it, he will probably need help in overcoming the addiction.

If he is just dabbling in it and asking his wife to join him, she can be a major factor in his abandoning it, if she is willing to give herself to him like they were newlyweds. That, after all, is what he really wants. He just doesn't quite have the nerve to tell her that.

Keep Going

I think there is one more thing we can learn from looking at Vashti. It is that, usually, life goes on. Many years after the events recorded in the Book of Esther, Vashti was in a position of honor and respect as the mother of King Artaxerxes.

Sometimes you hit a bump in the road, things just don't go the way you planned. Don't throw up your hands in despair. Trust God, read His Word, sing His praises, try to do right, and keep going. After all, what does the Lord require of us, according to Micah 6:8: to do justice, love kindness, and walk humbly with Him. Not perfection, not perpetual success, merely to do justice, love mercy, and walk humbly with Him.

Sometimes it's more than a bump in the road. Sometimes we skid on the ice or have some fool cut right in front of us, and we find ourselves exchanging insurance information with someone after a fender bender. Trust God, read His Word, sing His praises, try to do right, and keep going. Do justice (don't try to defraud the insurance company), love mercy (don't aim a lot of acid recrimination against the fool), and walk humbly with your God (remembering He's in control, not you).

There are times when we survive by the skin of our teeth, but the car—representing life here, as I'm sure you've figured out—is totaled. We seem to be back at square one, having not passed Go or collected two hundred dollars. Trust God, read His Word, sing His praises, try to do right, and keep going. Do justice, love mercy, and walk humbly with your God.

Once in a while there seems to be death and destruction all around us. The car goes right over the cliff, people are killed, planes crash into towers, children who are too far away for us to give them the dinner we didn't eat starve. Do all the same stuff. Right after you cry.

This paragraph from Eugene Peterson's, *A Long Obedience in the Same Direction*, speaks to this:

> Every day I put hope on the line. I don't know one thing about the future, I don't know what the next hour will hold. There may be sickness, accident, personal or world catastrophe. Before this day is over, I may have to deal with death, pain, loss, rejection. I don't know what the future

holds for me, for those I love, for my nation, for this world. Still, despite my ignorance, and surrounded by tinny optimists and cowardly pessimists, I say that God will accomplish His will, and I cheerfully persist in living in the hope that nothing will separate me from Christ's love.[1]

Even in the midst of (and especially after) disaster, there will be good gifts from God in which you can rejoice. Vashti had at the very least, her son, the king (sort of like the American classic, *My Son the Doctor*), who was loyal to his mom and took care of her. The sun will always rise, and sometimes it will color the clouds incredible shades of pink and violet.

Psalm 30:5 says that mourning may last for a night, but joy comes with the morning. There will be a bird singing outside your window, a child laughing somewhere, a friend calling to see if you are OK, and, at the end, there will be our Lord, smiling, with open arms, saying, "Well done, good and faithful servant."

My prayer for us all is, "Father, please help us to be respectful of even the difficult people in our lives and daily renew the hope in our hearts that the worst this world can do to us cannot separate us from your love. In Jesus' name, amen."

DISCUSSION QUESTIONS

1. What did you think of Vashti the first time you read the Book of Esther?

_____

_____

_____

_____

_____

_____

2. Did you vote for "courageous saint," "rebellious shrew," or "no clue?" Why?

_____

_____

_____

_____

_____

_____

3. If you had to choose one, would you rather be Esther or Vashti? Why?

_____

_____

_____

_____

_____

_____

4. Have you ever purposely or inadvertently put someone in a position where they felt shamed?

_____

_____

_____

_____

_____

_____

5. Where have you (or would you) draw the line between submission and taking a stand for righteousness?

_____

_____

_____

_____

_____

_____

6. Reread the Eugene Peterson quote on page   in this chapter. How close does that come to describing the way you live?

_____

_____

_____

_____

_____

_____

CHAPTER 10

SUMMATION AND REVIEW

Christ encourages us to pattern our lives after his. In this way we can become spiritually enlightened. The most important thing we can do is to meditate upon the life of Christ.

Many who have attended church all their lives have not been affected by it. They do not have Christ's spirit. If you really want to understand and enjoy the words of Christ, you must attempt to live like him.

What is the point of a scholarly discussion on a deep subject such as the trinity, if you lack humility? Deep conversation will not make you holy. God is pleased by a pure life. It is better to FEEL contrition than to know its meaning.

If you knew the entire Bible by heart, and were familiar with all the philosophers, what good would it be without the love of God, and his grace?

Here is the wisest thing you can do: forget the world and seek the things of heaven.

—Thomas a Kempis,[2] 1700's

The apostles themselves, who set on foot the conversion of the Roman empire, the great men who built up the middle ages, the English Evangelicals, who abolished the slave trade, all left their mark on earth, precisely because their minds were occupied with heaven. Aim at heaven and you will get earth "thrown in"; aim at earth and you will get neither.

—C. S. Lewis[3] 1900's

Are you amazed at how seamlessly these two people's thoughts fit together? Through the ages, God has spoken to those who love Him, and the words are different but the message is the same. Across the centuries their thoughts fit together like a hand in a glove, but their styles of expression are as varied as the people themselves. Like a good teacher, God keeps telling us the same thing in a new way till suddenly we "get it."

We are all of us alike in one respect. Every single Christian has something she can teach and lots to learn. Even the newly saved can share the fact that there is salvation available. The longer you walk with the Lord the more He will give you to share and the more you will realize that there is no end to the depth and richness of what is yet to be learned. If you ever start thinking that you have it all down now, you'd better get really scared and fall on your knees to ask for wisdom and a broken and contrite heart.

Proverbs says that the fear of the Lord is the beginning of wisdom. It is your awe of His "unplumbable" depths of knowledge and omniscience that is true wisdom not whatever snippets and crumbs of common sense and good advice you may have picked up while walking with Him. Guard against thinking you are wise in any other sense but that.

People who have not come into relationship with the living God through Jesus Christ sometimes see what appears to be a striking divergence between what they think the Word of God is saying and what they see when they look at mature Christians who are giving everything they've got to God and leaving the results to Him.

They may get the idea from Bible passages about our all being part of one body and from teachings that say we must die to self because it is not we who live but Christ who lives in us, that we ought to look very homogenous, and that if they choose to accept Christ, they would lose all their individuality.

Yet when they look at Christians, they see a wild and woolly mix of startlingly unique individuals.

They see J. R. R. Tolkien and C. S. Lewis flying on their imaginations into incredible worlds of fantasy and dragging a lot of the world after them—believers and unbelievers alike.

They see Brother Lawrence practicing the presence of God in an infirmary kitchen in the Middle Ages. They see Mother Teresa pouring every ounce of her being into the saving and serving on the streets of Calcutta the least of God's kids. They see some of us riding our spiritual "three-wheelers" through the world with obvious joy and others weeping and praying for the peace of Jerusalem.

They see Dorothy Sayers, Elizabeth Goudge, and Bodie and Brock Thoene writing wonderful fiction that lifts the spirits and inspires the minds of their readers. They see James Dobson creating a far-flung ministry to help people turn their hearts toward home.

They see Paul of Tarsus and Chuck Colson making big, wide, dangerous U-turns on the freeway of life, leaving behind everything that was important to them before to gain the privilege of telling people about Jesus of Nazareth. They see people in large groups praising God with abandon and others praying all alone. They see people worshipping in very formal church services and others praising God without restraint.

'How can this be?' they ask themselves. Aren't they all supposed to be conforming to the one vision? No! It's God we're seeking to be like, and He is big and wide, and as colorful as a prism, working different ways with different people. He didn't make all the plants or animals alike, but when He looked at them He said it was "good."

Lewis says that we are not fully ourselves until we allow ourselves to be put in the spot that God created us for. Not the spot that God created for us. The spot was there first. God crafted each one to fill a special place and responsibility in His plan. When you allow Him to fit you into that place, then you are truly free! All of the one-of-a-kind, seemingly screwy characteristics that God gave just to you are liberated.

You don't have to worry any more about what the world thinks. Romans 12:2 tells us not to be conformed to the world but to be "transformed by the renewing" of our minds. I once heard a speaker say that another rendering of the Greek word for "renewed" could easily be "exchanged." That's what God wants. He wants us to give Him all our old shabby ways and let Him exchange them for His ways.

The step of obediently laying it all down at His feet, not knowing what He'll do with it, is quickly followed by the part where God hands it all back, cleaned up, oiled, and newly painted. You become more truly yourself than ever before. All these lessons from Esther have really been about learning to lay it down, giving up "rights" in order to be granted freedom.

Why do you suppose we so often miss the best stuff in the Christian walk? Why do we more often feel like we're on a forced march rather than on a jubilant three-wheeler ride? Why do we fail to hear Him saying, "Lay that down. I have a surprise for you, but you're going to need empty hands to take it"? I think one reason is that we're not really paying attention.

> I turned to talk to God
> About the world's despair;
> But to make bad matters worse
> I found God wasn't there.
>
> God turned to talk to me
> (don't anybody laugh).
> God found I wasn't there—
> at least not over half.
>
> —Robert Frost[4]

Have you ever tuned anybody out? The attentive expression remained on your face; you didn't want to hurt their feelings, but you really weren't hearing a word they said? It can be accidental, sometimes your mind just wanders. But it can also be purposeful; they are rambling on about things that are meaningless to you, and you just mentally go away. God never does that to us, but we do it to Him all the time.

Sometimes we do it at the early stages of faith. We sort of have an inkling He's there, but we don't want to be made uncomfortable or to change anything, so we try to ignore Him. It can also be after we have come to a saving acceptance of His great gift of salvation through Christ. What a relief! Now we're safe, let's get on with our lives. "I heard You! I'm saved! Leave me be!"

It can even happen at a more mature stage. Having let God change our more obvious flaws—do away with our most egregious sins—we settle back in a self-satisfied deception that we are all done. Read this wonderful bit from *Mere Christianity* by C. S. Lewis.

> Imagine yourself as a living house. God comes in to rebuild that house. At first, perhaps, you can understand what He is doing. He is getting the drains right and stopping the leaks in the roof, and so on: you knew those jobs needed doing, so you are not surprised. But presently He starts knocking the house about in a way that hurts abominably and does not seem to make sense. What on earth is He up to? The explanation is

that He is building quite a different house than the one you thought of—throwing out a wing here, putting on an extra floor there, running up towers, making courtyards. You thought you were going to be made into a decent little cottage: but he is building a castle. He intends to come and live in it himself.[5]

He stands at the door and knocks, but if you refuse to let Him in, He won't make you into a castle against your will. If you tune Him out—don't study His Word, don't take time to read the great books that men and women of faith have written that will lift you and inspire you, don't take time to praise Him or talk to Him in prayer—how can He bless you? You will just have to struggle along as a slightly dilapidated cottage.

Think a moment about whether there was any spot in this book where God used His highlighter to convict you of something. What part of your house has He been working on? Maybe it didn't happen for everybody. Don't make it up. It's entirely possible that I missed something He was telling me to say that would have touched you. (There's a reason why this "tuning out" thing is clear to me.) A good way to do this is to flip back and review the questions at the end of each chapter, jotting down anything that stands out.

- Chapter one:

- Chapter two:

- Chapter three:

- Chapter four:

- Chapter five:

- Chapter six:

- Chapter seven:

- Chapter eight:

- Chapter nine:

How Do You "Tune In"?

In the course of this series of lessons, we looked at a lot of everyday life lessons, all derived from the Book of Esther. We discussed the importance of being loyal and faithful and about ways of counting the cost before we act. We investigated God's attention to detail and the fact that when He tells us something, we should write it down. We explored the concept of leading by example and strategies for not letting the small stuff spoil your joy.

We thought about our motives and how important they are, and we wondered whether, indeed, we have been put exactly where we are "for such a time as this." We tried to find some lessons about Christian marriage and about hope by looking at the inscrutable Vashti. We talked several times about the importance of studying the Bible.

How does all this apply to not tuning out what God is trying to whisper in your ear? I think the answer is in Second Samuel and that it has to do with obedience. David spent his youth protecting his father's sheep; then after killing Goliath, he became a mighty warrior in King Saul's army.

Saul, jealous of David's success and worried that the people would make David king instead of him, plotted to kill him and drove him from the court. David hung out in the wilderness with his family and a bunch of misfits and ne'er-do-wells until King Saul was killed in battle. At the opening of Second Samuel, he has been king for some time. He has waged war, established his kingdom, and been successful. Now read 2 Samuel 11:1: "In the spring of the year, the time when kings go forth to battle, David sent Joab, and his servants with him, and all Israel; and they ravished the Ammonites, and besieged Rabbah. But David remained at Jerusalem."

Remember what I said earlier? You can't make much progress if you have one foot stuck in the past. David was sitting on his laurels believing his own press. Why should the mighty king take care of details like waging war? If he had been where he was supposed to be, temptation would never have come upon him. What was he doing taking his leisure on the roof where he could look over and see Bathsheba taking her morning shower and be sorely tempted by her beauty? He should have been with his troops!

Obedience—doing your duty—, being where you are supposed to be, will often keep you from being blindsided by temptation. It probably seemed to David like an innocent enough indulgence. "Joab's an able man. I think I'll let him handle the battles this spring. I've worked hard pulling this kingdom together. I could use a little rest." But it started snowballing, like the "little white lie" you tell. Suddenly, you find you've been spinning bigger and bigger whoppers to cover it up.

Just as not being where you are supposed to be can open you up to the devil's spider web, the more you struggle, and the more stuck you get. Being in the right place, counting the cost, being faithful, hanging on to your joy, etc., etc. can help you tune your ears to God's "channel."

1. Have you ever gotten into trouble or fallen into sin because you weren't where you were supposed to be?

_____

_____

_____

_____

2. Has it ever happened because you failed to do what you knew you should?

_____

_____

_____

_____

3. Is there something God's calling you to right now that you are resisting?

_____

_____

_____

_____

Here's one last bit about adjusting your antenna to God's "station." I'm sure you've heard the phrase "junk in, junk out." It refers, of course, to computers and is an accurate description of how they work. If you enter the wrong address in the map program, the resulting directions will not get you to where you want to go.

I have a theory that we can learn a lot from watching how computers work, because they were designed by human brains and must therefore reflect them to some degree. I know for a fact that I have tremendous stores of data in my brain, but as I age, the search engine for retrieving them seems to have developed a glitch. Sometimes the most intricate details pop right up, and other times it will take days to think of some plant's name. "Oh, yes, that's a …, it's an uh …, well, it's a member of the same family as that other one that looks a lot like that …, you know, it's a …, phooey!"

Just like the computer, what we put into our minds will be what we get out. If we put in filth and degradation, ugliness and disrespect, that is certainly what will come out when we open our mouths, whether we intend it to or not. God doesn't run His ads on that page. If you want to get "e-mail" from God, you'd better have a filter in place to keep that interference out. We have three main ports of entry for data: what we hear, what we see, and what we read.

A lot of the things we see that pollute our minds and create static on the God channel, are on TV. Those of us who grew up watching the "innocent" shows of the fifties have a tendency to think all this trash on television is a new phenomenon, but the subtle influencing of our minds away from thinking like God thinks has been there from the beginning.

I Love Lucy was one of the funniest shows ever made, but have you stopped to think how often Lucy and Ricky lied to each other? It all seems so harmless, and it would all come right in the end with Ricky saying, "Ohhh, Loocy!" and giving her a big hug. In a real marriage, those lies would have led to a breach of trust that would have taken years to heal.

At the present time, there's not much you can watch on television that doesn't parade immorality and situational ethics before your eyes. My husband and I both enjoy football and other sporting events on TV, but if there were children in our home, I would have to think up creative ways to watch even those because of the commercials.

One fairly obvious idea for weaning yourself and your family away from the tube (especially if you are really addicted and just can't function without the light and noise) is classic movies on tape. Eventually, you should try to be doing other things, but replacing *The Simpsons* with *October Sky* or *National Velvet* is a start.

What we hear seems simple enough too. Proverbs 4:14-15 says, "do not enter the path of wicked, and do not walk in the way of evil men. Avoid it; do not go on it; turn away from it and pass on.". Where are you hanging out that you hear things you didn't really want on your hard drive? Don't go there! How about the radio? I hope you haven't tuned in the likes of Howard Stern, but some of the hosts on contemporary music stations, while not in the same league with Howard, are still saying things we'd be better off not hearing. Tapes in the car, Christian radio, or the classical music stations are good alternatives.

Now, finally, we're to the port of entry I really want to concentrate on, because this one is completely discretionary. We can overhear things we wish we hadn't. We can be thrust into places and situations where we see things we wish we hadn't, but we can choose what we read, and reading can play a major role in helping you pull away from the things you don't want to be hearing and seeing.

I read almost like breathing. I've always got one of my current books with me. Standing in line at the grocery store, waiting at the doctor's office, even gassing the car, I've always got my eyes in a book. You'll be glad to know I do draw the line somewhere: I don't read while driving, not even at stop signs.

About fifteen years ago, I realized that while a lot of my favorite authors were great, and pleasing to God, I was also reading a lot of stuff that put pictures in my mind God didn't want there. It was a wrench to give up the likes of Jonathon Kellerman and Marcia Muller, but as I got farther away from them, I began to realize that a lot of what they wrote was just a trick.

It was a formula they had worked out to keep you on the edge of your chair with no character development and little time spent polishing the language. They were craftsmen, not artists. It was like the difference between a piece of furniture from K-Mart and a thing of beauty created by a master carpenter. Once the habit was broken, I didn't miss them.

You can't reread these people's books. Once you have seen the twist at the end and know where the plot is going, there is little else to be gleaned. I have, on the other hand, read each of my Elizabeth Goudge books many times. My two favorites are *The Rosemary Tree* and *The Dean's Watch*. Here is a passage from *The Rosemary Tree*[6] to give a hint of what I mean. Harriet is a very old woman, confined to her room.

> It was supposed that if Harriet had a soothing nightcap the last thing, it helped her go to sleep.
>
> Harriet disliked hot milk and longed for a cup of tea instead, but she liked to foster illusions about her sleeping. Also it was part of her code in illness to accept whatever was done to her, given to her, and said to her in the way of treatments,

medicines, food and advice, with equal gratitude, dislike it or not.

Illness was admirable training in the creative art of grateful acceptance. Pain was just pain, and heavy, but Harriet believed that pain gratefully accepted took wings, went someplace and did something. She based this belief on her experience of hot milk, which just drunk down lay heavy on the stomach, but gratefully accepted, settled well.

Harriet was not a naturally pious woman, and she was not sentimental. She merely went on results.

Harriet, and the young people who love her and try to serve her, can become part of you. Yet the story isn't even about them. It's a love story about two other people in the village where she lives.

1. Which "port of entry" do you need to guard more closely?

_____

_____

_____

_____

_____

_____

2. Read Philippians 4:8–9. How does that apply here?

_____

_____

_____

_____

_____

_____

3. How could you apply the principles of Philippians 4:8–9 to your daily life?

_____

_____

_____

_____

_____

_____

At the end of this chapter there is a reading list of fiction, non-fiction, and biography. It is far from exhaustive, but nothing on it will harm you, and a lot of it, in all three categories, will challenge you to think more deeply.

My prayer for us all is, "please, Lord, keep us drawing closer and closer to You and farther and farther away from the world. Tune our antennas to hear Your voice. We want to pay attention. We want to be transformed."

Reading List

Devotionals

The Business of Heaven, C. S. Lewis
Nearer to the Heart of God, Bernard Bangley
My Utmost for His Highest, Oswald Chambers
The Art of the Soul, Joy Sawyer (not really a devotional; more of a weekly reader, as there are fifty-two, three-page chapters)

Nonfiction

The Hiding Place, Corrie ten Boom
How Now Shall We Live? Chuck Colson
The Case for Christ, Lee Strobel
The Case for Faith, Lee Strobel
The Case for Creation, Lee Strobel
The Valley of Vision, Arthur Bennett
Teaching a Stone to Talk, Annie Dillard
Dancing to the Heartbeat of Redemption, Joy Sawyer
The Light and the Glory, Peter Marshall and David Manuel
From Sea to Shining Sea, Peter Marshall and David Manuel
Sounding Forth the Trumpet, Peter Marshall and David Manuel

Experiencing God, Henry Blackaby and Claude V. King

The Book of Virtues, William Bennett

Our Sacred Honor, William Bennett

What is a Family? Edith Schaeffer

The Mark of a Christian, Francis Schaeffer

Pensees, Blaise Pascal

Imitation of Christ, Thomas a Kempis

The Attributes of God, A. W. Tozer (anything else by Tozer)

A Long Obedience in the Same Direction, Eugene Peterson

Praying in the Spirit, John Bunyon

Pilgrim's Progress, John Bunyon

Mere Christianity, C. S. Lewis

The Screwtape Letters, C. S. Lewis

The Problem of Pain, C. S. Lewis

The Four Loves, C. S. Lewis (anything else by C. S. Lewis)

Deliver Us from Evil, Ravi Zacharias

Darwin on Trial, Philip Johnson

The Divine Conspiracy, Dallas Willard

Walking on Water, Madeleine L'Engle

Biography or Autobiography of:

Detrich Bonhoefer

Fanny Crosby

Ben Carson

Mother Teresa
Chuck Colson
Amy Carmichael
(The list is endless, check the bookstore.)

Good Authors of Fiction

Elizabeth Goudge: *The Bird on the Tree, Pilgrim's Inn, Heart of the Family, The Rosemary Tree*, and many others. (Some may be out of print but can be found used or maybe on the Internet.)

Dorothy Sayers: all the Lord Peter Wimsey mysteries and anything else

Flannery O'Conner: anything (most still in print)

C. S. Lewis: *The Space Trilogy, Chronicles of Narnia, Pilgim's Regress*

Charles Dickens: Revisit this old master, where evil always gets its just desserts and virtue is eventually rewarded.

Bodie and Brock Thoene: *Twilight of Courage, Vienna Prelude*, and the other six in that series. The Zion Chronicles series and many others.

Jan Karon: The Mitford Series

J. R. R. Tolkien: *The Hobbit* and *The Lord of the Rings* trilogy

Stephen Lawhead: medieval adventure

John Grisham: *The Testament*

Madeleine L'Engle, *A wrinkle in Time,* and many others.(No these are NOT just for children)

Francine Rivers, *the Mark of the Lion* trilogy, and many others

Good Writers of Lighter Fiction (not an exhaustive list)

Jack Cavanaugh
Terry Lee Hatcher
Catherine Palmer
Cindy McCormick Martinusen
Beverly Lewis
Bonnie Leon
Francine Rivers
Linda Hall
James Scott Bell

There are *many* writers of Christian fiction. Some are more skilled than others. These are ones I have enjoyed, but check out the Christian bookstores *and* the library. The more people ask for Christian fiction, the more likely the libraries are to buy it.

ENDNOTES

Chapter 1

1. Webster's New Collegiate Dictionary, 2nd edition., s.v. "loyalty", "faithfulness."
2. Lewis, C. S. *Mere Christianity*. London: Pte. Ltd., 1942, 1943, 1944, 1953).
3. Swindoll, Charles. Esther. Nashville: W Publishing Group, a division of Thomas Nelson Inc., 1997.

Chapter 2

1. Peterson, Eugene. *The Message*. Colorado Springs, NavPress, 2002.
2. Charles Colson, *Chuck Colson Speaks*. Urichsville,OH: Promise Press, 2000.

3. Tada, Joni Erickson. *More Precious than Silver.* Grand Rapids, Zondervan,1999

4. Swindoll, Charles. Esther. Nashville: W Publishing Group, a division of Thomas Nelson Inc., 1997.

5. Lewis, C. S. Christian Apologetics. London: Pte. Ltd. Extracts reprinted by permission.

6. Evans, Tony. The Urban Alternative, 1-800-3222. www.tonyevans.org.

7. Bunyan, John. *How to Pray in the Spirit*, ed. L. G. Parkhurst Jr. Grand Rapids: Kregel Publications, 1991.

8. Focus on the Family. family.org.

Chapter 3

1. Blackaby, Henry. *Experiencing God*. Nashville: Lifeway Press, 1990.

2. Peter Marshall and David Manuel. *Sounding Forth the Trumpet*. Grand Rapids: Revell, a division of Baker Books Company, 1997.

3. ten Boom, Corrie. *The Hiding Place*. Grand Rapids: Baker Books, 1971.

Chapter 6

1. Lewis, C. S. *Mere Christianity*. London: Pte. Ltd. 1942, 1943, 1944, 1953.

2. Bangley, Bernard. *Nearer to the Heart of God.* Orleans, MA: Paraclete Press, 1998.

Chapter 7

1. Stroebel, Lee. *The Case for Christ.* Grand Rapids: Zondervan Publishing House, 1998.

Chapter 8

1. Jeremiah, David. *The Prayer Matrix.* Sisters, OR: Multnomah Publishers, Inc., 2004.

Chapter 9

1. Peterson, Eugene. *A Long Obedience in the Same Direction.* Downers Grove, IL: Intervarsity Christian Fellowship, 1980.

Chapter 10

1. Kempis, Thomas A. (1380–1471). *Imitation of Christ.* Chicago: Moody Press, 1984.
2. Lewis, C. S. *Mere Christianity.* London: Pte. Ltd., 1942, 1943, 1944, 1953).
3. Edward Connery Lathem, ed. "Not All There", 1936. Lesley Frost Ballantine, *Ten Mills: The Poetry of Robert Frost.* 1964.: Henry Holt and Company, 1969. Reprinted by permission of Henry Holt and Company, LLC.

4. Lewis, C. S. *Mere Christianity*. London: Pte. Ltd., 1942, 1943, 1944, 1953).

5. Goudge, Elizabeth. *The Rosemary Tree*. London: Van Rees Press, 1956.

Bibliography

1. Johnson, Philip. *Darwin on Trial*, Downers Grove, IL, InterVarsity Press,1993

2. Colson, Chuck. How Now Shall We Live. Wheaton, Tyndale House, 1999.
   "Somebody's Trying to Make a Monkey out of You." David T. Moore. www.Moore On Life.

To order additional copies of

Life Lessons from
Esther

Have your credit card ready and call:

1-877-421-READ (7323)

or please visit our web site at
www.pleasantword.com

Also available at:
www.amazon.com
and
www.barnesandnoble.com

Printed in the United States
78550LV00001B/41

9 781414 104096